HEALING AFTER INFIDELITY

THE ULTIMATE GUIDE TO RECOVER A PEACEFUL STATE OF MIND WHEN TRUST IS BROKEN IN YOUR MARRIAGE AFTER AN AFFAIR, WHETHER YOU ARE THE VICTIM, OR THE UNFAITHFUL PARTNER

Susan Courage

© Copyright 2020 - All rights reserved.

The content contained within this book may not be reproduced, duplicated or transmitted without direct written permission from the author or the publisher.

Under no circumstances will any blame or legal responsibility be held against the publisher, or author, for any damages, reparation, or monetary loss due to the information contained within this book. Either directly or indirectly.

Legal Notice:

This book is copyright protected. This book is only for personal use. You cannot amend, distribute, sell, use, quote or paraphrase any part, or the content within this book, without the consent of the author or publisher.

Disclaimer Notice:

Please note the information contained within this document is for educational and entertainment purposes only. All effort has been executed to present accurate, up to date, and reliable, complete information. No warranties of any kind are declared or implied. Readers acknowledge that the author is not engaging in the rendering of legal, financial, medical or professional advice. The content within this book has been derived from various sources. Please consult a licensed professional before attempting any techniques outlined in this book.

By reading this document, the reader agrees that under no circumstances is the author responsible for any losses, direct or indirect, which are incurred as a result of the use of information contained within this document, including, but not limited to, — errors, omissions, or inaccuracies.

TABLE OF CONTENTS

INTRODUCTION 6

CHAPTER 1 HOW TO REACT TO INFIDELITY 10

CHAPTER 2 THE POINT OF VIEW OF THE INJURED PARTNER 18

CHAPTER 3 THE POINT OF VIEW OF THE UNFAITHFUL PARTNER .. 26

CHAPTER 4 FIGHT DOUBTS AND FEARS 30

CHAPTER 5 CONFRONTING YOUR PARTNER TRANSPARENTLY 34

CHAPTER 6 HOW TO DECIDE WHETHER TO STAY TOGETHER OR BREAK UP . 42

CHAPTER 7 HOW TO ACT IF YOU WANT TO STAY TOGETHER 46

CHAPTER 8 HOW TO TRULY FORGIVE 52

CHAPTER 9 HOW TO REGAIN TRUST 58

CHAPTER 10 HOW TO RETURN TO SEX 62

CHAPTER 11 HOW TO ACT IF YOU WANT BREAK UP 68

CHAPTER 12 HOW TO LOOK BEYOND 74

CHAPTER 13 HOW TO CALM THE EMOTIONAL STORM 78

CHAPTER 14 HOW TO KEEP YOUR SELF-ESTEEM STEADY 86

CHAPTER 15 HOW TO FEEL ALIVE AGAIN 92

CHAPTER 16 HOW TO DEAL WITH NEW RELATIONSHIPS AFTER SUFFERING A BETRAYAL 100

CHAPTER 17 WHY NOT SEEK REVENGE? 108

CHAPTER 18 WHAT TO DO IF YOU WERE FORCED TO LEAVE 112

CHAPTER 19 HEALING 116

CHAPTER 20 THE MOST POWERFUL CREATURES ON THE PLANET 120

CHAPTER 21 ENDING THE SELF-BLAME, GUILT, AND REGRETS 126

CHAPTER 22 LET GO OF THE STORY 132

CHAPTER 23 BECOMING THE BEST, ME 140

CHAPTER 24 ACT, DON'T REACT 146

CHAPTER 25 TRANSFORM FROM BEING A VICTIM TO A VICTOR 150

CHAPTER 26 SECRET TO HAPPY MARRIAGE 156

CHAPTER 27 THE NEED FOR PARTNERSHIP 164

CHAPTER 28 SEEKING HELP 170

CHAPTER 29 HOW TO INVEST IN THE MARRIAGE 178

CHAPTER 30 CHOOSING HAPPINESS 184

CHAPTER 31 TURNING CONFLICT INTO WAYS TO GROW 190

CHAPTER 32 RE-STORY YOUR LIFE 194

CHAPTER 33 COUNSELING AND THERAPY 198

CONCLUSION 202

Introduction

If you have been betrayed by a spouse or long-term partner, the concept of looking at him/her as a two-year-old might feel like a way to excuse their choice to lie to you and to pursue a secret relationship away from home.

If you are ready to dig deeper into understanding infidelity so that you can start living again, keep reading as I share how I started to accept that the affair had happened in a similar way we come to terms with natural disasters.

Like a hurricane or an earthquake, Mark's infidelity was something I didn't ask for and it had nothing to do with me, yet I still had to face the consequences. The Five Gifts gave me tools to help me heal. They are introduced in a few pages "Infidelity as an intentional disaster".

There are other tools and resources that led me to a place of greater peace only a year after D-day. I realized that I cannot force Mark to be enthusiastic about being with me and I have to live with this notion without fear.

It doesn't matter how "By the book" I do everything including eroticism, building the bridge for him to cross, as stated by Esther Perel in Mating in Captivity, or being in "my element", building my career. If he's going to fall for somebody else, he's going to fall for somebody else.

This is something I started to look at without the fear I once felt as the daughter of an unfaithful. It was a life changing perspective.

Having a clear exit plan, in case we decided to go our separate ways, eliminated relying on the constraint "until death do us part" that had created uncertainty and anxiety in me, as a wife.

I learned that, in marriage, we have to monitor our feelings, our goals and our commitment to one another regularly. Nobody had prepared us for midlife crisis or for the challenges of a long-term relationship with regards to the things that are left untold.

Nobody had prepared us for midlife crisis or for the challenges of a long-term relationship with regards to the things that are left untold.

Spouses or partners follow the story they learned from their own family without even being aware. There are so many subtle messages and assumptions as we face "adulting" with a life partner. We are not equipped with tools to properly communicate our needs to our spouses. Some of us don't even know what we want because we haven't been trained to look inwards.

Dr Margaret Paul, an author and psychotherapist, has devised six steps for becoming a loving adult to your inner child. I recalled how Mirror Work helped me soothe my inner child. In the Six Steps to Inner Bonding, Dr Paul explains how we must be willing to look inwards to be able to heal.

Once we are compassionate and loving towards ourselves, we will be able to pour love outwards and forgive the betrayal and other shortcomings in our loved ones.

If we can stand on our own two feet, we do not fear that the erotic connection that serves as an indicator of how we're doing in our marriage might change at any time. On the contrary, the notion of impermanence can make us more aware of the benefits of today.

The notion of impermanence can make us more aware of the benefits of today

Understanding that uncertainty is the only real thing to expect, unlike the "and they lived happily ever after" we were poisoned with, is key to a healthier life. We heard all those stories with happy endings yet there was never a follow-up to show exactly how the couple faced the challenges that would arise beyond finding each other and being able to live together.

Since I cannot prevent infidelity from happening again, I decided to do the second best. I have worked on accepting every day as it comes and on focusing on the good in my life while I'm here. We are not going to live forever, and I want to make the most of what I have. I want to be happy. And you? I'm sure you do too.

Chapter 1
How to React to Infidelity

Infidelity has its roots in many different factors, both in the relationship, and on the personal plane. There is always a warning, a sense that something is wrong. But that doesn't justify the infidelity. There are always problems that precede the cheating. So, the most common problems that precede infidelity are all very similar, however, the first thing you will notice is the absence of a strong emotional connection. That connection may never have existed, or, alternatively, collapsed over time, because the couple paid insufficient attention to their differences or to the problems in their relationship. Infidelity is often a symptom of repressed dissatisfaction, unresolved conflicts, lack of communication, lack of passion, misunderstanding, and the tenderness or love they don't receive in the relationship or the marriage.

This is the first problem, if something is bothering your partner the honest and preferred course of action is to talk about that problem. Infidelity is not an option.

The partner who chose to cheat reflexively places the fault on their partner. This, of course, is at least an acknowledgment that someone is being hurt. While most people have the opportunity to cheat, they overcome that urge, knowing that they will live with that truth for the rest of their life. Imagine having kids and cheating your partner. How will that affect them? Ultimately, the children suffer because someone decides to be selfish. Does that seem right to you? Of course not; it cannot be right. That is an example of pure selfishness. Do you understand the thought process of a person prone to infidelity?

When the infidelity is revealed, the trust disappears, weakening the emotional and sexual attachment of the partner. Disbelief and the shock of discovery are universal reactions. Sadness, depression, feelings of negative self-worth, and intense anger toward the partner who committed infidelity are typical feelings that accompany such a crisis. Even those who have had doubts become distraught when their worst fears are realized. At the moment of discovery, each partner reacts strongly, yet differently. In the first days and weeks, both are overwhelmed with feelings of tremendous loss, guilt, and shame. A cheated partner may react with tears, even rage. The situation may manifest in physical reactions, such as nausea, headache, sleeping and eating problems. On the other hand, the partner who has committed the infidelity, often has a feeling of shame and remorse for what has been done, and a fear that the cheated partner will not forgive them. The injured partner has lost the positive image of their life partner, and the belief in a secure, committed relationship. The partner who has committed infidelity has lost their secret love, and also faces the potential loss of the marriage or the relationship.

Who is to blame here? We are not animals! We must resist this urge at any cost. It is very simple, when you love someone you don't hurt them. Once again, I will make this point—there is no justification for infidelity. If something doesn't suit you...

leave the relationship. You will end things in a humane and proper way. Otherwise, you are nothing but a coward. As I said, every relationship is a highway. If you don't like it, take the next exit.

A person experiencing infidelity has lost trust in their partner, and they want to be assured that the relationship with the third party will terminate. They also want answers to questions regarding that relationship. A person has a long memory when it comes to a partner that had a love affair, that lied, that concealed infidelity, and they often visualize the details of the sexual relationship of the unfaithful partner. The partner who has committed infidelity can respond with complete honesty, or with silence, because they are ashamed, and don't want to hurt their partner further. Whether or not reconciliation will occur depends on several factors, the most important being, 1) the motivation to preserve the marriage or relationship, 2) the willingness to communicate honestly and solve problems, 3) the willingness to apologize and repent, and, 4) the willingness to change, which sadly, is not always possible. That is the simple truth, so stop blaming yourself. Remember that the other party always had another option available.

1. You Must Know This As Well

Infidelity does not mean that a relationship or marriage is "doomed". Although infidelity is one of the most difficult experiences of a loving life, it is possible to recover, and develop a relationship with greater trust, increased commitment, and deeper love. Couples can learn to rebuild their relationship and make their relationship even stronger successfully. Forgiveness is a difficult process, both individually and collectively. It takes work, on both the personal and the partnership level, to regain that lost confidence, and it requires both partners to exhibit a lot of patience.

2. What Is Essential?

To begin this process, the transgressing partner must completely cease contact with the third party and notify the deceived partner of any attempt by the third party to contact them. Honesty and loyalty will help to restore confidence in the relationship. In practice, it is useful for the deceived partner to know, in detail, the daily obligations and schedule of the unfaithful partner. This will remove all doubts regarding how the transgressing partner is spending their time. Serious conversations in which the reasons for forgiveness should be repeated and reinforced and expressing sincere repentance for what has happened are obligatory. The apology of the partner who committed the infidelity must be sincere and must include an acceptance of personal responsibility for the infidelity. Taking responsibility for your role is also very important to the process. This does not mean that both partners should bear equal responsibility for infidelity, but rather identify the factors that influenced those events, so that they can prevent a similar occurrence in the future. The best way to prevent infidelity is by constantly investing the time necessary to ensure the foundations of a marriage or relationship.

3. How Serious Is Infidelity?

Apart from illness and death, nothing but infidelity creates such tremendous suffering. No matter how much time passes, perhaps as long as the marriage itself, there will still be difficulties in understanding why it happened. Why? How? We spin in circles. This is not a healthy—ever.

People respond in varied ways to the mention of infidelity, from bitter condemnation to resigned acceptance, to excitement and even approval. Infidelity may be ubiquitous, but how it is understood depends on the time and place of the drama. In the modern world, the love affair is primarily experienced through the damage it causes. It is always viewed through the lens of agony and the suffering caused by betrayal. The agony is that infidelity is not only causes a loss of confidence, but also the collapse of the high expectations of romantic love.

It is a shock that makes you question your past, your future, and your identity. The swirling emotions that emerge from the discovery of an affair can so overwhelm, that psychologists associate it with the symptoms of trauma; obsessive negative thoughts, excessive anxiety, numbness, alienation, unexplained anger, and an uncontrollable panic.

The damage inflicted on a deceived partner is only one side of the story. Modern culture is much more sympathetic to injured partners. But not enough attention is paid to the meaning and motives of the affair, and what we can learn from it. The affair can teach us a lot about relationships or marriage—what we expect, what we think we want, and what rights we think we have. They reveal our personal and cultural views on love, lust, and commitment—views that have changed dramatically over the past one hundred years. Once again, if love exists—infidelity is definitely not an option.

4. What Is Crucial?

We still want everything that the traditional family is supposed to provide—security, reputation, property, and children, but now, we also want our partner to love, want, and be interested in us. We should be the best of friends, and passionate lovers. We want our loved ones to offer us stability, security, predictability, and reliability. And we want it to last. What is the point of the story if your partner doesn't have the same perception of love? It's like trying to play a note on an old piano. You can hit the chords, but you will hear no music. The hammer is hitting a string that doesn't exist.

5. What Is The Point Of Everything?

At weddings, vows are made, and oaths to eternal love are sworn. Infidelity should never happen in the case of true love because all the reasons for it have been removed, and a perfect balance of freedom and a sense of security is achieved. But infidelity happens in good marriages and in bad. The freedom to leave the relationship or to divorce does not make the infidelity obsolete. Since it is possible to leave, why do people cheat?

6. And Why Do Happy People Cheat?

"Old wisdom" would say that adultery occurs when something is missing in the relationship or marriage, because if you have everything you need at home, as modern marriage promises, you should have no reason to go anywhere else to find happiness. Infidelity is a symptom of a failed relationship. So, whatever the problem is, if you love someone, there are always two paths; the right path and the wrong path.

7. Is Infidelity In Any Way Justified?

Theoretically, we all know that infidelity is immoral. However, there are situations where certain people will consider adultery to be justified, assuming that they are not the ones who are deceived, but it is very difficult to justify such an act.

For example, a woman might consider infidelity as okay when a woman cheats on a man that is tormenting her, especially if he cheated on her first. A man who cheats on his wife and gets away with it, may be considered by other, like-minded men, to be a hero of sorts. This is an example of pure hypocrisy. Another example is when one of the partners refuses to have sex for some reason or for no reason at all. After all, the partner being denied has to do something about their natural needs. Really... trying to solve this problem with a loved one and complaining is not considered an acceptable way to meet those needs?

8. And, What Is The Real Justification?

The real justification doesn't exist. People cheat out of selfishness, because at that moment, they are satisfying their own needs (for sex, for attention, for feeding their ego), which, in the moment, is more important than the fact it will hurtful to their loved one. It is also possible that they feel justified engaging in the infidelity, because of some perceived hurt, but this is still not a valid excuse. If the relationship no longer works, it is better to end it than to cheat. If there is no sex in the relationship and one does not want to end the relationship, then those needs must go unfulfilled, thus avoiding harm to the person you are in relationship with.

The shortest answer to the question of when infidelity is justified would be—never. There are other ways to deal with the problem that do not involve a betrayal of trust.

Chapter 2
The Point Of View of the Injured Partner

Dealing with difficult emotions has been one of the greatest rocks I've picked up on my journey through betrayal trauma. I've grown in my ability to take care of myself emotionally. I've learned so much about feelings: what they are and how to deal with them. I'll share with you this pebble I've put in my pocket.

A problem of betrayal trauma is that I feel an emotion faster than I know why I'm feeling it. If I don't slow down, the emotions will leak out and cause damage.

I've never been good at slow.

When the worse thing I could imagine happened, it broke me into a thousand pieces. God then began His work to put me back together in a healthy, strong, and whole way. He took all those pieces and started rebuilding me piece by piece. A huge part of putting me back together in a strong and whole way was emotional management and learning how to deal with hard feelings.

What was this simple task supposed to accomplish? How could this help me deal with my heavy emotions?

When I first started doing mindfulness, I thought there was no way I could look at my feelings as something disconnected from me and NOT me. It was very discouraging. But the more I watched my feelings come and go, the better I got at it. It was like a muscle that grew stronger inside of me. Honestly, my ability to look at my emotions like that gives me a lot of freedom.

One of the benefits of mindfulness is that it teaches me to disconnect myself from my feelings. I'm not my feelings. Emotions come and go upon me, but those feelings are not who I am. When I see emotions in that way, I'm better able to go back and see where my emotion came from and validate why I'm feeling that. Then I'm not judging or shaming myself but taking care of myself while I'm feeling and sitting in that emotion and either work to let it go or wait for it to pass. And through this process, I remember my supreme value and worth despite what I'm feeling.

My feelings tell me something. Sometimes, my feelings tell me that injustice has happened and it's not right. Sometimes, my feelings tell me that I'm angry at another for what they did to me. Sometimes my feelings tell me that I'm sad. I listen to my feelings and what those feelings are telling me. These feelings give me insight about myself. They help me create connections about myself and my world and who I am and what I need. These insights are precious. Once those insights are gained, then the feeling sometimes goes away or is less intense. Those feelings finally did their job and told me what I needed to learn.

I've learned to be kind to myself in my feelings. Being kind to myself looks like me not getting upset with myself that I feel angry. It looks like me not shaming myself for my feelings.

I've learned to validate myself. Validation looks like me acknowledging that there was a reason why I felt that way.

That validation allows me not to stuff down my feelings. The truth of why I feel the way I do often sets me free.

When feelings sometimes sit on me and won't release, I have to practice a lot of self-care until they let go. Sometimes, I know why I'm feeling a certain way, but I still can't get past it. At those times, I do everything I can to work through the steps to take care of myself, acknowledge and validate, rinse and repeat, until they let go.

As you work to recover from betrayal trauma, you gain tools to deal with whatever emotions come up. Safety comes from knowing you have the tools to deal with whatever emotions come up.

Mindfulness and Breathing

First, I breathe in and out. I close my eyes and focus on my breathing. When the body feels a fear, we shorten our breath and breathe faster. Our body goes into fight or flight. My daughter told me that studies show that when you're stressed, you stop breathing, so if you choose to get your body breathing again, then you can decrease your heartbeat and your reaction.

As I choose to control my physical body and deepen my breath, my brain starts to slow down and not just react. My brain thinks it's safe because I'm choosing to calm it. This takes a lot of practice. The more I did mindfulness, the better I became at calming myself and grounding myself. Breathing began to be the beginning of the new ground I would stand on. Breathing would form the building blocks of a new security found only in myself and in my God.

As I breathe, I focus on the present moment. At first, this was so hard for me. My mind was racing, and I couldn't stay focused very long. But I got better at it. And it definitely helped me.

If I have time, I do guided meditations with mindfulness. Sometimes, when I go to a place of fear, my thoughts go wild and I think about things that aren't necessarily true. It's important to fill my mind with truth when I feel afraid. Guided meditations put truth back into my mind. I can cling to that truth instead of dwelling on things that I think are true but aren't.

When I've calmed down enough, I try to see where the emotion came up. As I walked back through what happened, I found the moment where the emotion came upon me. I can validate myself and say, "Yes, that would be a difficult place. I can see why it came." This allows a space and moment to validate myself. That validation feels good. The feeling that came is real. What I'm feeling is real. The pain is real. The anger is real. The emotion is real. I validate, validate, validate. I don't stuff it down. It's true; I do feel that way and there's a reason why.

Validation

One of the difficulties of betrayal trauma for me was that for a long time, outside sources told me my feelings were silly and unfounded. Even when I found out that everything I felt WAS true and real, I still had to relearn not to shame myself in my own emotions. Because I had been treated that way by others for so long, it was difficult to do. I had to learn to stop shaming myself.

If my body is telling me it's afraid by a sudden increased heart rate, and I keep telling myself that it's dumb and shove the fear down inside me, the fear won't go away but will continue. I'm ignoring a natural defense mechanism in myself.

If I'm feeling angry, it's telling me a boundary of mine was violated. If I ignore how I feel, I lose valuable information about what my body is telling me.

Others let me down by not validating how I felt but I won't do that to myself. I won't ever again shame the emotions that I feel.

Facing the Emotion

If I'm validating myself, then I'll need to face the emotion and be curious about why it came up. Maybe it wasn't something that happened but a memory that came up that caused emotion. I face that memory. Facing it looks like writing about that memory or reliving it in my mind. This is another more profound way to validate how I feel. I remember or write about it again from all the senses: what it smelled like, what the colors were in the scene, what the different feelings were, how others were behaving. I write about it all. Sometimes, a memory and the accompanying emotion might keep coming up. So, I might have to write about it multiple times. The important thing is not to stuff my emotion or memory. I need to keep the emotion flowing like a healthy stream of water, not a stagnant, smelly pond that just sits inside me. Also, if it's too hard to do that on my own, I'll need a therapist to help me.

Emotional Regulation in the Heat of the Moment

How do I deal with emotions when I'm facing them at the moment? First, I think this just takes a lifetime of practice. I have to choose to be still. If I'm staring anger in the face, I start by breathing. I also get myself out of the situation. I know I'll burn hot, so I don't even mess with my weaknesses. I get out. I can't deal with it at the moment. It's kind of like a shark, once those eyes roll back, there's no stopping its fierce jaw from clamping down with a considerable force of pressure. This is me when anger or other hard emotion comes. I have to cool off before I incinerate. So, first, space is critical for me.

Another part of this emotion principle is that if I act out in emotion, the person is most likely to hear the anger and not my actual pain. I don't want to act out because then the focus will be on my misbehavior not their misbehavior. And to be honest, I don't think that people even care to hear how you feel at the moment. They're most likely in survival mode too.

Fight, flight, or freeze modes come when we don't feel safe. I don't let my feelings escalate to fight mode. It only hurts me. Yes, I'm justified to be angry, but if I fight back with anger, it will only hurt me. I fight back in different ways using clear language and working hard to disconnect from their crazy making. I can stand in my truth, which is how I feel, and let it stay there. They won't fix it or change, but I can at least say my thoughts in a rational way.

I'm better able to "fight" this way as I prepare for "battle" by working out my anger beforehand and envisioning myself staying calm. If a topic light me up, I do intense work on my side to figure out why I have so much emotion there. Then when I go back into the arena of discourse, I'm better able to leave anger at the door so that the conversation can be focused and kept on my pain and the actions that are causing the pain.

Crying

I cry. Crying gets out my emotions. It seems like its nature's way to get out what's on the inside of us. Sometimes, when the pain gets so bad, I sob and cry so hard that my shoulders ache afterwards.

I give myself space to be messy with my emotions. I cry in the woods where no one can see me. I cry in my closet where hopefully no one can hear me. I cry in my car. I cry in the therapist's office. I cry with safe people.

My hard cries can be ugly, so it's good to have a space to be authentic and pour out my ugly emotions.

Chapter 3
The Point Of View of the Unfaithful Partner

If you are the one who strayed and turned your affection to someone other than your spouse, you need to decide whether you want the relationship to go in. Look at the reasons leading you to stray. Take responsibility for your actions, be accountable, be patient, and practice honesty with yourself and with your spouse. Be loving and understanding through the hurt, the anger, the regret, and the intense jealousy until you find a way to solve the issues permanently.

One of the questions that a person (especially the one cheated on) can keep asking him/herself is if the infidelity meant falling out of love. Honestly, anything involving human beings is hardly ever black and white. People have different personalities; thus, life is complicated. The complex nature of human beings can make a reasonable person look like a bad one and vice versa. For instance, a person who cheated because he/she felt deserted can appear like a terrible person while it was the first time. That complexity can make love feel dead for a while such that a person goes to look for the beautiful feeling outside the relationship.

Most people who have affairs are actually in love with their primary partner, and a good number of people having affairs are not cheaters by nature. If one were entirely out of love with the leading partner, they would leave rather than have an extra affair. Some off these people in an affair are not liars and betrayers, so we cannot classify them as bad people. True, their deeds are wrong, but everyone is human, capable of making catastrophic mistakes. We all do; we all will.

What I find most interesting is that people being in an affair is not about wanting a different relationship, instead, it is about wanting a difference in the primary relationship. Every marriage and relationship changes with time, and consequently, our needs might get left behind. We can forget things such as connection, love, validation, nurturing, and intimacy as life gets complicated with other tasks. These complications are not a valid reason for people to cheat but understanding the things that fueled straying can help to fix a relationship.

Cheaters Will Always Be Caught

Cheaters will be caught, be it today, tomorrow, next year or ten years from now. And that will not end well. A cheater does not have to be caught red-handedly with solid proof. No, it could be in a way he/she never imagined a most minute way, almost too cheap. There are behavior changes that accompany cheating:

- A spouse may start treating his/her partner better or worse.

- A wife may change certain habits; for instance, start working out more. However, this is not always the case.

- A person may start to lie unnecessarily.

- There might be unexplained calls and messages.

- Sudden changes in moods, among others.

There might be legitimate reasons for these behaviors, but if one suspects something is not adding up, an investigation might ease the mind. In the end, a cheater will be caught because that is nature. The changes become too prevalent to hide. Even when the cheater has covered his/her tracks, the other person will get to a point where he/she wants more and more time. Consequently, one will observe more calls and messages without clear explanations. The emotional rift following an affair is very hard to miss. There will be something that will signal the other that something is wrong. Sometimes, the cheater can sell him/herself out by being too careful. Either way, cheating will make life complicated no matter how smart one is.

Typically, a cheater who is caught has cheated more than once. A one-time cheater can get away with his/her actions but will confess one day due to guilt. Someone who cheats often will at one point of the other get too comfortable especially if he/she has done it continuously without being caught. Because of the continuous deceit, the deceived partner may have a hard time forgiving the cheating partner. The offender might not even show remorse for his/her actions since it has become a norm. Too much cheating might render the cheater shameless and guiltless. Without remorse or guilt, the cheater appears not to care about the spouse at all.

If the guilty person, however, confesses because of shame and guilt, it is less likely that he/she has cheated for long. That does not necessarily mean the cheater has not cheated for long, but confession creates an excellent platform for forgiveness especially if it is accompanied by regret, remorse, and empathy for the innocent partner.

Keep this rule of thumb in mind: A cheater with a conscience, empathy, remorse, and empathy for the partner will regret hurting the relationship thus is more likely to commit to rebuilding what he/she broke. In other words, infidelity does not have to be the end of your relationship, rather, it can be a learning point from a stupid mistake. A right partner will promise never to cheat and keep his/her word.

If you have caught a spouse cheating, and he/she does not feel worried, shocked, remorseful, regretful, sorry for hurting you, or awful because of being caught, you are probably in a wrongful relationship. That person might feel bad for being caught but not for his/her actions. Anyone who shows genuine pain and guilt for being caught and is willing to rectify things in the relationship has a more substantial chance of working things out. You will need to do a lot to rebuild the relationship, but the affair can be a thing of the past.

Chapter 4
Fight Doubts and Fears

The aftermath of a discussion with our partner can be just as painful as first discovering the affair. We may feel that, far from helping us achieve a sense of closure, we have more questions than ever.

We need to keep in mind at this critical juncture that everything we feel is valid, everything we feel is justified. The pain, the rage, the grief, the fury. The bitterness and the sheer shock. We were not the ones that upended one of the most sacred tenets of our relationship, we have a right to feel however we want to feel. There is no denying this.

That said, as tempting as it may be to lash out at other people, be it our spouse or anyone that catches us in a bad mood, our actions more often than not have lasting consequences. We must proceed with this in mind at all times.

The key part of this is that at almost every step of this journey, to whichever resolution we decide it must lead, we will need our heads more than our hearts. Our hearts are already busy dealing with the emotional turmoil. While they can be good judges in other situations, this is the time to hand over the reins to our mental faculties, shake out any cobwebs and think out a solution.

At this stage, what we're managing the most is our pain. We've had the initial shock, and we've just sat down to talk over the issue with our partner. They've told us more details than we thought we wanted to know and left some lingering questions that they didn't feel ready to answer.

Our minds are unquestionably in turmoil and it is easy to get sucked into this tidal wave of potent emotion. It is tempting to give in to it as a form of targeted release. It is oh-so-tempting to take action, whatever it may be, so that we can deal with the situation as is. The problem is that doing so will only provide a temporary solution to the situation at hand. It is vital to remember that throughout the ordeal, whatever form it takes and however it plays out, we must never choose a temporary solution.

This could be a good time for us to return to our threefold plan from earlier:

Stop. Breathe. Think.

Stop. You've had the conversation and you've heard their side and all that you've heard is rolling over in your head, screaming to be attended to. Ignore them for a bit. They will be here when you return and unfortunately, before you can move past it, you will have to return to them.

Breathe. Take a deep breath, retreat to your happy place. Just take a moment to clear your head and then…

Think. Think now of ways we can take all this roiling emotion, all the pain and adapt ourselves to it. Moving forward, this pain will be part of us, and we have to accept that. Knowing that the pain will accompany us for the better part of our near future, we must be practiced in making clear and clever decisions, even with the constant hurt. It is vital, in this time, to find our inner strength.

Again, ways to do this are not set in stone. We are all unique and different human beings, and we could differ from one another in how we find our strength. In this regard – and only in this regard – it is not entirely too bad of an idea to vent. Some people appreciate a change of scenery, some people prefer the company of a close friend or relative with whom you can just sit and be or you can cry your heart out to. Some of us may want to break a few plates.

On occasion, we may want to find somewhere quiet to scream ourselves hoarse just to vent. That's okay. The essence of it is just to let the pain flow through us and to acclimatize ourselves to its presence so that whatever actions we take in the future are taken with a clear head. This is where we take that moment to be as loud and obnoxious as we want.

As with everything, however, keep in mind that we will likely have to deal with the consequences of whatever we do in this period. Be sure that we don't hurt anyone else during this venting-period, break valuable relationships, wreck the priceless family jewels, or throw out the baby with the bathwater.

Our attempt to ease off the pressure inside our head should do that, and only that. We don't need to give ourselves more problems to deal with.

We need to seek out the things that make us feel lighthearted and are good for distracting us for extended periods, like a waking nap that lets us refresh without stress constantly hovering over us. Yoga can be helpful, as is the opposite end of the spectrum, such as getting into fast-paced sports or other kinds of physical exertion. Never rely on clichés. Whatever works, works.

Being sucked into creating origami figures for an hour or two at a time has as much virtue as letting our kids talk us into playing video games. If it provides mental breathing room, grab at it with both hands and knock off some time every day to get it done. Of course, these should still be reasonably healthy habits, or even habits where we break even at the very least.

It's okay to have a glass of wine every night after dinner, curled up on the couch watching our favorite TV shows. It's not okay to have a hangover every morning that makes us late for work.

Life goes on with or without us, and we must not let our spouse's faults lead us off our chosen paths in such a fashion. It's good to break down every once in a while, to cry it out, to sob into our pillows. It's also good to pick ourselves up and be as strong outside as we are inside. To remind ourselves that nothing has diminished us as individuals with hopes and dreams. As human beings.

Chapter 5
Confronting Your Partner Transparently

Say Enough

There comes a point in time when you need to cease thinking about what you are losing and begin to think about what you will get by leaving the relationship. This is because, the longer you stay in the relationship, the harder it will be for you to get your serenity.

If life was similar to romance movies, the one we fall in love with would be the one to make us happy. However, in reality, things tend to go differently. We fall in love, let our guard down, and someone takes advantage of this to hurt us multiple times. Yes, it is fine to fight for a relationship, but when the relationship is a toxic one, you need to learn when to say enough. This is because if you don't, the damage it will cause you down the line can be irreversible.

Love can seem like an addiction, and like all addictions, there are healthy and unhealthy ones. Relationships, as we have covered in earlier are also the same. And harmful relationship addictions can break down a person in the most negative ways. A relationship that is toxic and filled with emotional abuse, hostility, danger to you, and other toxic behaviors, are the most difficult to leave. In theory, they should be easy to walk away from, but practically, this is not the case. And this is why it is essential for you to walk away as fast as possible, because the longer you stay, the harder it is to let go.

There are instances when the signs are apparent. These could range from cheating, physical, and emotional abuse, continuous criticism, among others. Sometimes the signs may be as mild as lack of intimacy, perpetual heartache, and loneliness.

It is hard to leave any relationship, including toxic ones. It requires a tremendous amount of strength and energy to say enough and let go of a toxic relationship. So, what do you need to do to help you through the process of saying enough?

Stay in the Present

It is tempting to live in the memories of your relationship. For instance, how the relationship used to be. The same applies to living in the future. That is hoping that things in your relationship will get a lot better or fantastic. However, if you need to find the strength to leave a toxic relationship, you need to live in the now or present. To do this, experience the entire relationship for what it is at that moment. Doing this will help you see how damaged or toxic the relationship you are trying to save is.

When you constantly look at the relationship the way it once was or the way you hope it would be, to convince yourself to stay, then there is a problem. See the relationship for what it is presently, and it will be less complicated for you to make your choice.

Have a Record

Keeping track of how the relationship makes you feel can be another excellent means of helping you decide. Keep a journal which comprehensively states everything you feel in the relationship. You need to include the day to day events of the relationship over a specific period. If you don't enjoy writing, it is also possible to take advantage of pictures to help you with this. Take a photograph of every vital moment in a relationship that brought out either a bad or good reaction from you. Do it for a specific period which could be 1 -2 months, or weeks, depending on what is suitable for you.

After the set period, go through your records and answer the following questions:

- Are the feelings mostly good or bad?
- How often do these feelings take place?
- Is there a pattern?
- Is it a continuous or rare occasion?
- Do you love the person you have become?

If you used pictures:

- Do you look happy or lively or drained out in them?
- Do you seem sadder than usual?

Providing answers to these questions can let you view the relationship the way it is. Without the excuses and paddings, you use to make it more appealing to yourself. In the end, you will see things with more clarity and make the right decision.

Observe What Your Body Says

The mind and the body are interconnected. The connection they both share is one that is quite powerful. If you block off the messages and signs that your mind or gut tries to tell you, then your body takes up the role. You will observe some feelings and signs in your body like tension and heaviness, among others. Also, the way it works will change.

To determine what your body is saying, ask yourself the following:

- Do I feel physical pain in my body?
- Is there a feeling of heaviness in my body?
- Does my body ache?
- Does it look like I am losing weight?

Providing accurate answers to these can help you see the relationship for what it is.

What Is Your Coping Mechanism?

Look within yourself; do you have any coping mechanisms to ensure you don't feel terrible? Or what behaviors have you adopted to help you in the relationship?

As opposed to not dealing with the terrible feelings that arise, try to examine them. When you deal with the pain you are feeling; you will get the strength, bravery, and wisdom you require to be able to say enough.

Put A Deadline in Place

When you hope something to improve in the future, it is not difficult to forget how long you have been waiting. To place a deadline, select a specific period, be it a few weeks, months, or even a day. You need to pick a deadline that you feel is ideal for you. During this period, do all you can for your relationship. Put in as much energy as you can into it until you exceed the period you have set aside for yourself. Then observe the results, and you will find the answer you need.

Get Out of Your Role

In all relationships, each partner picks up a role over time. This is more like a pattern which keeps the relationship going and allows each partner to maintain their behavior. This does not imply that you are responsible for being treated the way you are being treated, especially if the relationship is toxic one. However, it does mean that you have picked up a particular way of behaving that makes it easy for you to bear the unhealthy relationship.

In toxic relationships, there is a victim, and there is an abuser. You need to determine what your exact role is. Are you the rescuer? Or the one who keeps giving excuses for the other? Determine your role and try to get out of it. By changing the dynamic this way, it will ensure the unhealthiness in your relationship is more apparent, making it less complicated for you to say enough, and leave the relationship. At the very least, you may trigger a positive change in your partner.

Leave the Imagination Behind

When you fantasize about the possibilities of the future, it can result in you being tied down to a toxic relationship. Holding on to fantasies will prevent you from seeing things as they are. Because you believe things can get much better, as you have seen in your fantasies, you will keep trying until you can try no more.

The more you allow your imagination to rule you, the more you try to change your reality to match your fantasy. The same applies even if you are in an unhealthy relationship. Your imagination will push you to hold on longer than you usually should, even if the relationship is a toxic one. If the way you imagined your relationship was going to become a reality, it would have changed already. So, let go of the imagination, and you will see things for how they are, which in turn will give you the energy to say enough.

Defend your Well-being

By prioritizing yourself, you will indirectly give yourself the energy to fight for you. Everyone, including you, deserve happiness, but in most instances, you will have to fight for the joy you want. Give yourself a priority and fight to get the best treatment for yourself in a relationship. When you observe it is not something your existing relationship will offer you, you will get enough energy to walk away.

Stop the Excuses

It is perfectly normal for us as humans to give excuses for those we love. This becomes particularly heightened when we are in a relationship with that person. However, doing this excessively does not make one see the relationship for what it is and can make you stay longer than you should in a toxic relationship.

Search within yourself. Have you ever gotten what you desired from this relationship? How does your desire differ from what you presently have? Does it feel like you are being loved or treated right?

In a healthy relationship, even when arguments arise and we say and do things out of anger, you can still feel the respect and love behind it even during the hard times. Once you stop making excuses for your partner, you will be able to see the relationship more clearly and see it for what it is.

Unhinge Your Mind

If in your mind, you genuinely believe you can't leave, then it will be difficult for you to do so. Do not limit yourself by constantly believing that you can't leave. Change your mindset and tell yourself you can leave when you want to. Make your choices based on what you want, not based on what you think you can't do. By changing your mindset, you will get the strength you desire to make a decision that you truly want.

Take Courage and Make a Decision

Lastly, take courage and make your decision. And whatever you choose to do, ensure you own the choice you make, knowing you were responsible for making this decision. If you don't make a decision now, it may seem fine for a while; however, over time, it will keep you tied down, and without the strength you require to say enough and leave this toxic relationship.

Besides, note that if a relationship feels toxic and unhealthy for you, then it probably is. At this point, you can fight as hard as you can to fix your relationship. However, when you have no more energy to keep on fighting, you will see things clearly, as they are.

Every relationship goes through difficult times and can get past it. However, in unhealthy relationships, this cycle is repetitive, which makes it essential to either fix it, or leave as soon as you can. The decision to remain or leave an unhealthy relationship lies with you, but you need to be sure your reasons are the right ones when you do make a choice.

If you do decide to say enough and leave the relationship, you will need to learn the appropriate way to do so.

Chapter 6
How to Decide Whether to Stay Together or Break Up

Understand What Is Required If You Decide To Stay In the Relationship

If you decide to establish and maintain a relationship with a narcissist you should know that there will be a lot required of you. A huge amount of your time will be needed, and your presence will be demanded.

Yes, narcissists can express their love for you, but they will also require you to reciprocate that love or to at least express it profoundly in return. You see, you will have to assure narcissists to appease their anxieties.

There will be times when it will be like you need to give unconditional love. Well, sometimes that is exactly what a narcissist will want from you.

Some narcissists fear abandonment and they will do everything—and I do mean everything—to keep you with them. Well, that is if they have grown to love you. But remember that there will be many days when it will be like they are pushing you away.

They will be angry at you, they will put you down, and even insult you. Sometimes it will feel like the narcissist is pushing you away. But then again you'll be dragged back into loving arms.

Remember that they will be driven by this seemingly illogical need for approval. Because of that they will do things that will seem to sabotage your relationship. It's a cycle really—a crazy cycle of love and hate.

Nevertheless, there is no harm in trying to love a narcissist even if the one you're trying to love has severe symptoms of NPD. There will be people who will not understand why you're putting up with all the bad treatment.

Some would even say that your narcissist doesn't deserve you. And that is part of the package—there will be pressure within the relationship and there will be pressure from without.

Just remember that the bottom line here is that you chose to be in this relationship, not them. It's a gamble and you can't play it without being fully into it.

When you find yourself unable or unwilling to cut off a narcissist, there are other ways to protect yourself from the narcissist's manipulation and harmful behaviors. One of those ways is setting healthy boundaries. Healthy boundaries are necessary to protect yourself when interacting with other people. They represent the line that others know not to cross when dealing with you and create a divide between yourself and others. Boundaries are healthy for everyone, including married couples or parents and children. It is important to note that you can have a relationship where you tell each other everything but still have boundaries; the boundaries are behaviors you refuse to tolerate, not walls that you set up to push other people away. A healthy boundary may be expecting to be treated with a certain level of respect or insisting that you will not tolerate name-calling or other demeaning behavior. Most people would agree that not being called names is an acceptable boundary and will not cross it.

Maintaining Yourself

When dealing with a narcissist, you find yourself having to make plenty of concessions to avoid meltdowns or outrages. With narcissists, you often feel as if you have to choose between pleasing yourself or the narcissist. It's frequently easier to forego what you want than it is to deal with the backlash from the narcissist. It is important to make sure you maintain your sense of self during the process of dealing with a narcissist, and you need to be able to understand what the appropriate steps are to maintain yourself. You need to know when flexibility is useful or if setting boundaries will be a better course of action. You also need to understand when enough is enough so you can take a step back from the situation and disengage from the narcissist for your own physical and emotional safety. Learning these skills will give you a much better grasp of how to interact with a narcissist while minimizing damage for everyone involved.

Bending, Not Breaking

Just as the tree bends to the wind to keep from breaking, sometimes being flexible with your expectations is the best choice when it comes to dealing with a narcissist. Narcissists are stubborn by nature; they want everything to go their way and struggle to cope when things do not play out as they expect. The average person is much better at coping with small missteps in their plans without being tripped up, and sometimes, the easiest way to maintain yourself and your sanity is to remain flexible. If the concession is something you truly do not care about, it is likely not worth the battle of remaining firm. Pick your battles and let the narcissist have her way if you are indifferent.

Your self-awareness and self-restraint will be two of your greatest defenses against falling victim to narcissistic behaviors. Unlike the narcissist, you can recognize when you are wrong without sending your world shattering around you, and you can also restrain yourself when something does go wrong. You have developed proper coping mechanisms and have learned to handle stress in healthy, productive ways that do not worsen your problems. Remembering to utilize your self-awareness will keep you aware that you are angry or frustrated with the narcissist. This recognition allows you to be aware that you may be more prone to lashing out at the narcissist at that moment, which also allows you to utilize your self-restraint. You can remind yourself to stop, take a deep breath, and count to four before reacting to keep from impulsively lashing out.

Remember, by remaining flexible when applicable, you keep yourself from breaking. Your flexibility keeps you strong and able to withstand the difficult behaviors that come from the narcissist. Your patience will keep you firm as you encounter the same issues over and over, and your self-awareness will help you acknowledge your feelings so you can cope with them in a healthy, productive way.

Chapter 7
How to Act If You Want To Stay Together

You don't want to let go. You still have faith in the relationship. You wish to get your partner to forgive you and get rid of the resentment they have towards you, and you want to give your marriage a chance. This becomes difficult. The spouse can't seem to forgive you and can't get over the hurt they are feeling. The first step in rebuilding the relationship is to get over this hurt and resentment. It can be caused by your affair or humiliating them in public in some way, or due to some specific behavior that you displayed to them. The resentment towards you has something to do with what you have done to them in the past, and as a reaction to which they are still disrespectfully treating you. You may not have cared about their feelings. It can even be mental or physical abuse or lack of intimacy. People gets focused on stressful points in their lives and tend to neglect their spouse. They tend to shut down in front of you. They stop responding to you emotionally. There can be a lack of communication. One of the prime reasons that's causing these negative feelings to grow is lack of intimacy. This includes sex and also simple affection. Perhaps your partner doesn't want to touch or doesn't want to be touched or hugged or kissed. Sometimes spouses tell them that they are physically repulsed by them. This is the ultimate sign of hurt and lack of forgiveness. They may start to put other things ahead of you in the relationship. They feel other things are of a higher priority. It can be their children, other family members or friends, or even their hobbies, their business or their career. Ideally, the relationship must be one of the highest-ranking priorities in both people's lives. They may intentionally hurt you, and it may seem impossible for you to make them forgive you. They may be alienating you from your children or close friends or family members. Many may start to overspend. This is called financial sabotage. They intend to cause hurt to the other person after the other person hurt them. So, this creates a barrier between the two of you. It makes communication, trust and intimacy almost impossible. Therefore, you need to eliminate these barriers to move forward.

Another thing that may be triggered is that it causes you to behave in the same way. You may also start holding back and emotionally shut down. Check your partner's behavior and begin to analyze the pattern of resentment that they are displaying. This can give you clues on how to deal with it. First is when your partner wants to forgive you but doesn't know how. They recognize they are hurting, and they can't forgive you. They know their behavior isn't helping you, but genuinely don't know what to do about it. The way to know this is to ask yourself, is your partner aware that they can't forgive you? Does the inability to forgive make them feel bad? Does it appear that they seriously want to do something about it and they want to get over the hurt and resentment towards you. They are assuming some responsibility in trying to do this? The other type of resentment which is fairly common is when they don't want to forgive you. Even if they say they want to. They are in such a position that they use their apparent pain to punish the other person. They are saying you hurt me; I won't forgive you until you receive some punishment. So, they will punish you by staying hurt because they know that hurts you too. This is a very prevalent belief that people have. It is a way of maintaining control over you and the relationship. They are meaning to tell you how you feel, and this can take a destructive turn. You need to ask yourself, are they in a place where they can ever actually forgive you? You will be able to answer this easily based on their behavior and feelings and actions.

True forgiveness is removing all the pain and traces of the pain from the outer world and the inner world as well. To forgive, you need to completely get rid of all the remains of the pain surrounding what caused the hurt. It has to be unconditional. They have to say it doesn't matter what happens, they are going to let go and come back to you. It is acknowledging what happened and then sticking together and not letting the emotions of abandoning the person overpower you. This is the ultimate goal. It is achievable. Let's begin by stating that you must be sorry for what you did wrong, or whoever did wrong must have repented in their heart. That behavior needs to stop. If you had an affair, you need to stop everything you had with that person. You can't realistically expect not to be apologetic and your partner to forgive you. If the husband goes and cheats and the wife forgive, after half a dozen times, she stops forgiving and he wonders, why is she no longer forgiving me and is cynical. There has to be genuine remorse and a genuine want not to hurt the person anymore. If you do have a pattern of repeating what causes your partner to get hurt, you need to identify the cause that's stirring you to do it. You need to repair that element. It's not about dealing with forgiveness, it's about dealing with the pattern.

Certain myths need to be busted when dealing with the grey area of forgiveness in cases of infidelity. To think that time will heal, and the relationship will restore to its former glory—this is true to some extent. This can often be used as an excuse by a person not to do much. The person just wallows in self-pity. However, like any change, healing from hurt can be done quickly. The betrayed would need to have deeply and truly forgiven the other person. To do that, there has to be the right environment and the right mindset, and healing can come fairly quickly. You need to give it as much time as it needs. The process can be sped up depending on what you do and how you do it. Another myth is that it is up to the betrayed person to deal with. It's their problem, and you leave them and let yourself have time to soak it in and decide what you want to do. Having the unfaithful person take responsibility is certainly important. The problem is that if it's left to the victim alone to deal with, they might not know what to do and the timing is going to be based on their time frame.

You are not giving them any support. It should be explained that it is up to them to deal with the situation, but you are there to help and support them every step of the way. You are waiting for them to come back. But this shouldn't be misconstrued as you apologize all the time and crowding them. This will have a repellent effect. So, you need to find a balance to deal with the situation effectively. You are giving all of your power to them. What they need to get over the pain and hurt is some strength. You are making yourself weak, which is in turn, making the whole situation weak. There is nothing to pull them up here.

What can you do to try to get them to forgive you? Make sure not to take responsibility for their feelings. Your spouse needs to take responsibility for their feelings. They may not want to or may say that they can't. But true healing and forgiveness can never happen if it is not coming to them internally. The way to do this is telling them that you are sorry, and you are ready to take responsibility. You will make sure it doesn't happen again, but ultimately, it's up to you to be completely transparent. You can say you love them, and you want to help but you can't force them to forgive you. They need to take responsibility for that. Next is to forgive yourself.

You may have baggage on your shoulders and the guilt is eating you up inside and you may lose face and sleep. You did make a mistake. You are human. Everyone makes mistakes. This is not to negate the mistake in any sense. Accept and forgive yourself for that. You have assured them and yourself that it is never going to happen again. Make sure you are doing your best that it never happens again. Don't feel guilty. Guilt never does any good for anyone. Next, you need to acknowledge and resolve. Acknowledge to your partner that you did them wrong and tell them that is completely your wish to heal the relationship. It will be made better and will get back to what it was. Do this powerfully and firmly so that they know you mean business. At this point, it won't be advisable to ask them how they feel. They have done that over and over and revealed to you how sick they are feeling. Tell them how you feel. You are hopeful and willing to make amends. You resolve that things will change for the better and they will be better. The next step is to ask them to acknowledge that you are both human and you both are capable of making mistakes. Do this in a general and non-confrontational way. Tell them that you have acknowledged what you have done, and you resolve that you want things to get better. You have made mistakes, but they make mistakes too. You are not accusing them, but you are reminding them in a non-confrontational way. What you are doing is that you are getting them to acknowledge another side of what happened. There are always two sides to everything between a couple. The effect of what you are doing here will ideally diffuse some of the resentment and rationalize their fears a little bit. They might begin to see it's not fully your fault. You made a mistake and it's not the end of the world.

The last step lies in creating a positive healing environment. When we have a lot of problems in a relationship, that's what we are focused on. It just creates an endless cycle of problems, hurt, pain and misery. Now that you have acknowledged it's their responsibility to work on healing, and resolved to forgive yourself, this step is about moving on. You don't need to focus on this stuff anymore. Focus on creating a positive environment.

Chapter 8
How to Truly Forgive

Bitterness and unforgiveness were weighing me down. As long as I was holding on to justifiable resentment, I would suffer. There was bitter batter stuck inside the bowl of my soul that needed some cleaning out.

Forgiveness is how we let go. It's how we get free.

The Seven Steps to Create True Forgiveness
Step #1: Make the Decision to Forgive.

Your first step is to decide. Ask yourself, "Do I want to forgive my spouse?"

This might sound rather a strange question. However, it is somewhat surprising (until you understand human nature) how many people there are with a spouse who has had an affair who don't want to forgive them for it.

You might wonder why on earth someone would not want to forgive their spouse. If you are in the situation where deep down you don't want to forgive them, you may also wonder why you are feeling this way. The following explanation may help you to overcome this obstacle to forgiveness.

If you don't want to forgive your spouse, it is because there is a greater emotional benefit for you in not forgiving them than there is in forgiving them.

Step #2: Consider the Consequences of Forgiving vs Not Forgiving.

Whether you forgive or not forgive your spouse, there are going to be consequences. You need to consider very carefully what both the immediate and long-term consequences of each are, and the effects they will have on your marriage, your happiness and your life.

Let's look at "not forgiving" first.

If you continue not to forgive your spouse, you need to ask yourself - where will your marriage be in a year from now? Where will it be in 5 years from now? In 10 years? In 20 years?

Think of the pain that you're feeling right at this moment. What will happen if that continues for all that amount of time? What are you going to miss out on doing together with your spouse if you're carrying around all that pain and that hurt? In fact, will you even still be together? Can you see yourself down the track staying in the same position you are now and feeling all the pain that you're feeling and not forgiving them?

Also, how are you going to feel when you look back on all that time that's elapsed between now and then? What are you going to think about all the pain you had over all that time and how you lived your life because you didn't forgive your spouse? - How it kept you locked in a place of resentment. What effect will it have had on your life?

Imagine in 20 years, looking back and seeing that you still hadn't forgiven your spouse for what they did and thinking, "Wow, I spent 20 years - I spent my whole life - in this state of pain because I couldn't or wouldn't forgive them! And it was silly because the person who suffered the most was me!"

Looking on the other side, what would your marriage and life look like if you did get over the hurt if you'd found a way right now - and made the decision right now - to forgive your spouse unconditionally for what they did in the past. How would life be if you said, and "We're starting again? I'm going to trust my spouse totally. I'm going to forgive them unconditionally." If you did that, what would your life look like? And how would it look a year from now?

These are all things you need to think through because when you really start to look at and see the consequences of forgiving and not forgiving and the effect it has on your life, it's going to help you to realize how important forgiveness is. It will increase your greater resolve to forgive because it's not just for the sake of your marriage or your spouse that you want to forgive - it's for your sake as well.

Step #3: Uncover the Reasons for Your Hurt and Resolve Them.

Earlier, we talked about the feelings you may have had, but you need to think: "What specifically about what happened is causing me to feel hurt? What thoughts am I having? What's going on in my head whenever I think of what happened? What are the thoughts that come to my mind?"

Essentially, when you feel anything about anything - whether it be positive or negative - your feelings are based on some meaning you have attached to what has happened. That meaning is also related to beliefs you have about certain things and about certain areas.

Step #4: Realize your spouse is human.

Obviously, we're all human, including you and your spouse. But it's very easy to forget that, especially when you are feeling hurt by the actions of someone else. However, one of the things about being human is that we make mistakes.

Sometimes we expect that we will make mistakes, but nobody else can or should - particularly our spouse. But let's be real here: you make mistakes - and your spouse makes mistakes. By having had an affair your spouse has obviously made a mistake!

The more that you can see mistakes for what they truly are - that they're not intentional and they're not permanent - the more you can see that they don't need to be fatal and they don't need to affect you for the rest of your life unless you, of course, want to allow them to. And that's what these steps are all about, helping you to try and change what you allow into your mind - and therefore into your life.

Step #5: Uncover the real reasons why the affair happened.

Whenever a problem occurs in a marriage (or in any other area of life) it's usually an indication of some deeper issue. The problem is merely a symptom, it's not the cause.

So, it's important to ask yourself, "Are there any things going on in my relationship that aren't right and which could damage our trust, communication and intimacy?" What are the things (and there will be things) that are going on in your relationship that were conducive to allowing this affair actually to happen in the first place? This is about finding the real reasons why the affair actually happened.

Step #6: Refocus the blame.

You probably already know that blaming someone doesn't help improve any situation. You've might be told this or you've thought of it yourself, and you've probably also been told that you should stop blaming your spouse or blaming anyone in fact.

However, the problem, for all of us, is that even though we know we shouldn't blame, it's something we can't stop doing! So that's why, in this step, I'm suggesting that instead of trying to stop blaming anyone (whether it be your spouse or even yourself) what you do instead is that you refocus your blame. In this way you can still feel the emotion of blame (if that's what you want to do) but it's not done in such a way that it's going to hold you back from forgiving your spouse.

In practice, this means that instead of blaming your spouse, yourself, the 'other' person in the affair or anyone else, if you are going to put any blame anywhere, put it on your relationship. By that I mean acknowledge that there have been weaknesses in your relationship that's caused the affair to happen, and that all you need to do is uncover what those weaknesses are and fix them and you can not only repair your marriage but you can take it to a level that is much better than before.

There is great power in this. By focusing on the marriage, many couples have even been able to see an affair as a blessing! It has been the wake-up call for their marriage and forced them to uncover and address the issues that have been pushing them apart for some time.

Step #7: Create a Forgiveness Agreement.

This is an extremely powerful step. It's to create something that I call a "Forgiveness Agreement". This is actually a written document in the form of a true agreement. It is something that is well worth taking the time to do.

Chapter 9
How to Regain Trust

Trust is something we build over time; it is not freely given. It needs to be earned. Many of us have been betrayed in one way or another by parents, friends, teachers, or partners. It is hard to build up trust again, but we do manage. This is because we need to feel trust so we can rely on people around us and feel safe. Without the feeling of safety, we would be lonely and depressed.

We are confident that if you act on these steps they will help guide you in the direction of regaining lost trust and support you in the process of rebuilding your relationship.

Overcoming Blame

To regain trust, the first thing to do is to let go of any judgment. A Course in Miracles asks, "Would you rather be right or happy?" Quit thinking that what they did was somehow "bad" or "wrong." This kind of judgment only keeps you separate and distrustful.

Undoubtedly this isn't easy at first. After all, society is full of such judgments. Our entire justice system is based on this concept. So yes, we understand giving up your judgments that they did something bad or wrong may be very hard at first. Hard because most people believe giving up their judgment of someone's actions is the same as condoning what they have done. We assure you; it is not.

You can only let go of a judgment when you've been able to translate what they've done in terms of what they value. To help let go of any judgments it's important to know people only do or say things because they are acting in harmony with something they value, or as an attempt to meet some need.

Again, without specific examples it's impossible for us to guess what a person might value or what need they are attempting to meet. So, here's a hypothetical example of what we're talking about.

What a Liar

We agree that lying is not an effective way to create a satisfying quality of relationship or a very successful life. However, we want you to consider that there's a way to look at the situation that is less painful for you and has the possibility of creating a quality of trust that you long for with your spouse.

So, let's look at the situation from a new perspective. Your husband lied to you. Instead of being upset and angry that he's done something "wrong," you decide you want to discover what prevented him from telling you the truth in the first place.

Dig Deeper

Think about that. You can only understand this after you've come to realize he lied in service of something he values or as a way to meet some need.

And at this point, you don't yet understand what that might be. In this case, we believe you're upset about the lying because you value a quality of understanding and respect and fear losing that in the relationship. The fact of the matter is that telling the truth is at the heart of one of your core values: honesty. And because you value honesty, this it is exactly what we suggest you focus on establishing in your conversation with your husband.

If you're acting from a desire to create understanding and respect it's much more likely you'll accomplish this when you become curious about why he lied in the first place. It's likely you'll be able to see that his lying was not intended as a personal affront to you. Instead, when you understand what he values you can focus on improving your relationship and your ability to support him in getting his needs met in ways that work better for both of you.

Let's put ourselves in his shoes and try to guess what he values that prevented him from telling you the truth.

We'd guess that freedom of choice or autonomy is very important to him—he wants to be in charge of his life and decide where he goes. We'd also guess he was lying to preserve his peace or tranquility—he wants to protect himself from the upset that telling the truth might create, knowing that you don't like him playing golf as often as he does.

Ultimate Freedom

Once you're able to let go of the judgment that this person did something that you label as "wrong," you're then able to explore the situation effectively. You'll be able to see what prevented them from telling you the truth in the first place. Then the process of creating agreements about how to meet everyone's needs best can begin in earnest.

In this case, for you it would be about how to get your need for trust met and how to experience more honesty in your relationship, while at the same time helping him meet his needs for autonomy and his value for peace and enjoyment in his interactions with you—especially when he wants something other than what you want.

After you can let go of the idea that your spouse has done something wrong, you can begin to explore what everyone values, and then start figuring out ways that everyone can be satisfied—and everyone includes you.

Chapter 10
How to Return To Sex

Erotic recovery is very basic after a case of infidelity. Sex is a very basic part of a relationship, and every couple has to be intimately and erotically connected. Changing from the state of utter disconnect (emotionally and sexually) after an affair may seem difficult and even impossible to some extent more so if you are still in pain. However, if you decide to stay together, it will be necessary that you work together on your sex life. That is a vital part of your healing process.

Erotic recovery will encompass all your vitals, physically, emotionally, and psychologically. Intimacy will have to be considered thoroughly. Until you can move past the erotic difficulties of your relationship, the other person in the relationship will be in bed with you mentally. The bridge between the two of you may seem too wide, but at times, you will crave to be held again. Sex can be a way of recovering and feeling grounded a reminder of what life was like before the infidelity. Couples may find that the things they cannot share through words can be expressed through touch.

At the same time, infidelity can make you build walls so high to guard against any form of vulnerability. It will take time to make love the way you used to but be patient. Do not pressure each other if you are not ready. It is normal to worry about each other after an affair and wonder how the sex life will be.

At times, you will worry that the amount of sex you are having is not enough, while during other moments, you will feel like you are trying too hard. You should check if it is a genuine sex or you are just trying to manipulate your spouse. Talk to your spouse directly about your feelings. Make sure that you communicate about the readiness of having sex. If you are not ready, say it out loud.

There are things you need to know about sex life after a case of infidelity:

- Sex is an entirely different experience after infidelity. If a couple chooses to move on together after one of them has had an affair, it is a very major step. Recovering together is not an easy process, and this period will test every aspect of the relationship, including sex life. Getting back to the bedroom can be an effective way for a couple to rebuild their trust. However, sex can trigger a series of emotions, and the spouses need to be prepared for the harsh realities surrounding the post-affair relationship.

- You will not have the same relationship you had before. As you try to move on following an affair, you need to recognize that your past relationship is gone, and it is not coming back. Right now, you have to focus on building the new relationship, and that also includes sex. Do not assume that you will get back to the place you were. The sexual relation you had initially will have gone.

- You have to be patient until trust comes back. Sex is an incredibly intimate part of a relationship, and emotions run high. If you are still in the stages of recovery where emotions are highly unstable such that you cannot be around each other without getting angry, then you need to take it slow. Let the pressure reduce before you can rush back to the bedroom.

- In the right time and setting, sex can be a great source of healing. Sex can transport a couple emotionally and physically to places where words cannot go. At the right time, sex and spending intimate time together can help you restore the bond with your partner.

- You will have to reprioritize your sex life consciously. Sex was not something that needed a lot of force. It might not have been the best sometime before the infidelity happened, but you did not require thinking, rethinking, and prioritizing. However, you will have to make time for sex during the recovery period consciously. Remember that sex can be a healing experience when you are recovering from an affair. As such, you have to be ready for it, get good at initiating the action and have sex a priority. Get a little adventurous in the bedroom if need be. You will need to show each other the role sex is going to play in your new relationship.

- You will have to put everything on the table, including the taboo subjects. It will not be easy but choosing to move on means repairing every aspect of the relationship. You will have to talk about some of the sexual behaviors that lead to the affair. If sex were not amazing anymore, you would have to say it and look for solutions. Address whatever it is that lead to a breach of trust. Do your best to understand the cause of the affair. It will be difficult to open up at first due to the fear of hurting each other, but you will have to do it. You will also have to talk about what happened sexually during the affair. Total honesty is very important for trust.

- Look out for dysfunctions. Did you know that several people experience sexual dysfunctions after an affair? If it happens in your relationship, do not panic. Some women will have a hard time getting aroused after an affair, while men might fail to get an erection. These things happen mostly in the period of stress and turmoil. Therefore, you should not panic. Be patient with each other and understand the challenges you might be facing. If you encounter performance problems or if any sexual contact brings about bad memories of the affair, you might have to slow down and take some more time to heal.

Restoring the Intimacy

In some cases, the betrayed spouses will want to heal from the affair through having more sex. He/she might become what some therapists call super sex god/goddess. When the hurting spouse opts for such sex, it becomes great but not necessarily a good thing. The motivation is pain, and the betrayed partner is busy comparing and competing with the third party.

Remember that love is an action, and it is not about you only. So, if you are the one who cheated, and you tried something in the affair that you are not willing to in the marriage, then you have a problem that needs to be addressed. You need to ask yourself what the problem is. It could be guilt, depression, shame, or any other thing. Could it be the way your spouse kisses or his/her hygiene? Be open, honest, and have the dissuasion. One thing you can be sure of is that a marriage without intimacy is doomed to fail. As such, any struggles with infidelity should be addressed as soon as possible.

Chapter 11
How to Act If You Want Break Up

Did you ever have a need to open your mouth and speak? Did you ever feel stuck in silence? Clenched in a tight ball of worry and heartbreak and humiliating rejection? You're not alone. When I found out that my husband was cheating on me, I kept my mouth shut for over a year, and I did not tell a single soul. Why? So many reasons. All bad reasons. There's no good reason to hide your life from your loved ones. The reasons seemed important at the time.

I looked to him to comfort me, but he would not. I waited for him to remember who he was, but instead he became someone I didn't recognize. I stayed silent to protect his reputation, in hopes of reconciliation. I would have done anything to save my family. Anything. I stayed silent to make sure there was enough money in the bank. I didn't have a good job, and I was afraid. I stayed silent to protect my children from knowing that their lives were about to change drastically. My own feelings? I definitely felt some strongly unpleasant stuff, including anger, hatred, bitterness, and fear. I just held it all. Tried to stuff it down. Hid it. I wanted and hoped for my marital problems just to go away and magically, miraculously be fixed. I wished for the past.

At first, my own feelings, my own heartbreak, my own intentions, my own intuition did not matter, not even to me, because I felt like I didn't matter at all. I was all about reaction, every day for months. It was crisis mode for me, an emergency situation that lasted and lasted and lasted. I was being compared to another woman, and she had already worked diligently to beat me in a war I didn't know I was in. For a long time, I didn't even know she existed as a threat to my family. Turns out my husband was testing me without me knowing I was in a test. I failed that test spectacularly. It wasn't a fair fight. I didn't sign up for it.

Betrayal makes you feel less than good enough. It makes you feel like a huge failure. Suddenly, out of nowhere, your partner lets you know that you are unloved, even after a lifetime of assuring you that you'd be forever loved. All those deeply held heartfelt promises just vanish. You lose what you thought was true without knowing it was in the realm of possibility to lose it. And keeping that secret only digs you down into that dark hole further.

But. I slowly, eventually came around to this. What about me? Don't I matter? Doesn't my heart, my life make a difference in the world? Aren't I loveable?

And then, like a pinpoint of light in the dark, life started to get better. That small hope, that tiny glimmer, that light from God grew so fast in me that it took over everything else. The dark hole evaporated. Here is the hope that I found, and it is good.

I know God loves me. God's love is unfathomable, unlimited, and real. God's love doesn't falter, never fails. God is faithful. And if God loves me, then I am lovable. I matter. I am enough.

And so are you.

You are loveable. You matter. You are more than good enough. Actually, you are extraordinary. And now, you get to create the future that you want. You get the freedom to live without betrayal, without lies, without fear. You get to be authentically you, without apology, in every way. You don't have to make room for someone who is making you feel less than enough. You know the truth now. And you are an amazing and beautiful child of God, loved and adored by the source of all creation.

It is so freeing. It's freedom.

For over a year I shoved down every feeling and kept my mouth closed. My health suffered. I did a bad job at work. My heart physically hurt. My stomach hurt. I didn't sleep well. I dragged around, unsure of how to fill my waking hours. I had no interests beyond investigating my husband's affair and taking care of my kids. I stayed stuck looking back into the past, wishing for things to be different.

And then, it turned out, the wishing was pointless. There was no un-ringing that bell. I begged him to remember who he was, to stay, to love me, to keep his promises, to be there for the kids. I couldn't think straight. In all my failure, I still tried to be good enough. He moved out anyway.

So, then I finally, finally started to talk. Through phone calls, texts, and whispered conversations, I wrenched the truth out. It's Adultery. There's a mistress. My husband is cheating on me. He is leaving. He has in fact already left. He does not love me anymore. He maybe never did. I am home wrecked. He is moving out of state, closer to his mistress. There is no hope.

Decades of a shared life together are now down the drain. The kids, oh, my heart, I have to tell the kids. These are the things I finally said out loud. Sometimes I just had to say these things to myself to come to understand that this was my life now. Saying it let me loose from the terrible hold that silence had on me.

As long as I was silent, I was stuck recreating the same thought patterns over and over, nothing really getting any better.

Well. Now that I've had time to get my life back in order, I'm ready to tell the rest of the story. Because the sad part is over, and I am not sad anymore. Not even a little bit. But it took quite a lot of work to get here, out of the dark hole I was in. I'd like to try to help you find your way, too.

I want to tell you how much better it can be for you. I'd like you to know how grateful I am for every blessing in my life, and how leaving my marriage behind even though I didn't want to do so enabled me to create a new, healed, happy life full of freedom and choices. I have a completely different life. A good, happy, joyful life filled with every possibility, every satisfaction, and every good thing. And God's love has been the very best part of all.

And all, here's what I know for sure. God does not withhold the good things. People do, but God does not. God bestows favor, honor, and every good thing on you and me.

Now I remember that awful time, but I have learned not to dwell on it. Now, the present we are all in is full of more appreciation and gratitude than I could ever express. Now, the future that I hope for with God's help, mercy, love, and grace is absolutely full of possibility and blessings.

You can get to this wonderful place too. Don't wait another moment. Now is the time to work on you.

I need to show with my life how anyone can speak up, tell the truth about what is happening in your life, and move forward with the uplifted life that you can pursue after getting past betrayal. I know the future is hard to think about. Hard to start. It's hard to let go of everything you once had. But you can. You really have to. My intention is to help you turn your life's momentum towards hope, a healthy outlook, and a new path to move forward with love and light and uplifting words to the people who need it. That's you.

Chapter 12
How to Look Beyond

"Our work is love made manifest" is a compelling statement and describes precisely what I was looking for. How could I find the work that would manifest love in the world? Although I didn't explain it in this way early on, I was looking for what could I be in the world, what I could do to manifest love and make my life be about that.

Think about what that means: To know that what you do in the world makes a difference. That your work matters. That you matter. That you can be a catalyst for putting more love in the world. Is there anything our world needs more than that?

Remember the parable about the two wolves. Here are some ideas about how to perpetually feed your "good wolf," and how you feed it will uncover your genius if you look for it.

Read. Listen to podcasts. Watch TED Talks.

The world is flooded with skillful thought leaders from every culture and point of view. I couldn't possibly read all that is good in a lifetime, so you will never run out of great stuff. Some of my favorite thought leaders. Leaders include the following.

- Everything researcher Brené Brown writes or speaks about. Her TED Talks on shame and vulnerability transformed me in ways that nothing else could have.

- Thrive Global on Medium: a treasure trove of goodness.

- And no list of leaders would be complete without Oprah. Her website is chock-full of goodness and great interviews with other influential female leaders.

Turn your hurts and life experiences into healing for others.

Being able to use these experiences to lessen the pain and help others has given me purpose, meaning, and self-respect. Sometimes another person's pain can lead us to a higher purpose.

What have you learned in your journey that might be helpful to someone else? If you look, you will likely find many, many examples and stories.

I had a client that had survived rape. She struggled for many years to deal with her rage, sadness, and shame. She worked through these painful feelings for years to resolve them and was forever changed by the process. When we talked about her experience, I asked her if she had considered how valuable sharing her story might be for other women who have experienced rape and struggle to make sense of it. The idea lit her up. She went on to get trained to work as a rape crisis counselor, and she found her life full of meaning and purpose. Helping others healed her own heart.

What is the difference between the people who can summon deep meaning from their suffering while others are crushed by it?

A sense of awe, gratitude, and compassion are the keys to your direction.

When we talk about a "sense of awe," we're trying to describe a state of feeling connected to something bigger than ourselves. This is the emotional foundation to finding your purpose as it asks you to look beyond your own immediate needs.

Gratitude is also a foundational piece to finding your purpose. When we can look for and see that other people have made our lives better in so many ways, we are more motivated to look for ways we too can give back.

Compassion is the third leg of the purpose stool. I had a spiritual teacher who taught that the purpose of human life is to cultivate wisdom and compassion. We cultivate wisdom through our experience. Interestingly, it is often some of the painful experiences that teach us the most.

Cultivating your inner wisdom gives way to compassion. When we have experienced suffering, we can see it in other living beings, and, for most people, we carry a natural urge to help others not suffer. Why is that? Because we remember what our own suffering felt like. Soothing another's pain heals us from the pain we endured. Cultivation of compassion leads us directly to a meaningful life with purpose.

What is it that you have experienced, that you have a sense of awe about, find gratitude for, and has given you both wisdom and compassion? How can you use that to create a life of meaning and contribution for yourself?

Ask others who know you and love you what they see as your strengths.

You may be amazed at what comes up. When I had the chance to tell my friend that had given me such wise advice so many years ago on the heels of my financial disaster, he was amazed and thankful. He had no idea he had made such an impact on me. I told him that he had completely changed the course of my life for the better. His strength, insight, and willingness to see something in me that I couldn't see in myself at the time was life changing. It is no wonder he was wildly successful in business. Think about it: This was one conversation that completely changed the course of another person's life. It felt so good to tell him how much his advice and caring meant to me.

Chapter 13
How to Calm the Emotional Storm

Visualization

Take five minutes a day somewhere you know you will not be disturbed and close your eyes. Picture that your goal has already happened. You are here. You are healed. Picture what your life is like without the constant pain, anxiety, and obsessive thoughts. Really visualize what this is like and that it has happened.

What you are doing?

How you are feeling?

Where are you?

Make this a daily practice in the morning before you start your day. It will become the anchor to your healing path.

Self-Introspection: Time for a Self-Inventory

I remember once while on a date, my guy asked me if I would go on a hike with him. My instant response was "that's not really my thing." And right after I stated this, I remember thinking to myself, Why am I saying that? I have never even tried it. I love nature, so why wouldn't I try it? I realized when I got home that this was my old programming thinking and talking. The old Carmen thought about how she might break a nail or how her hair might not look good. This shallow, old way of thinking was not serving my highest good, so I needed to ditch this old thinking. Needleless to say, hiking to this day has become one of my favorite hobbies. It is an amazing, therapeutic activity that I will be doing for the rest of my life.

I realized at that moment that I needed to do an internal inventory check. I needed to dive into myself and analyze what else I had been putting these types of self-limiting beliefs on. I went on a quest to see what else I wanted to explore. It was amazing! It turned out I was a bit of a dare devil: I went sky diving and zip-lining a bunch of times, I tried every roller coaster known to man (and didn't like any of them), and I discovered how much I love doing physically challenging activities, traveling to culturally diverse countries, and exploring the jungle and archaeological sites. And I am still not done.

From that moment, I set out to inventory the most important parts of my life, my career, spirituality, relationships, and so on, and I was able to become crystal clear on what I wanted and was able to put together goals and intentions to get me what I desired.

Now let's do an inventory of the four most important parts of your life: home, career, relationships, and spirituality (or edit these however you see fit), and begin to define the wants and don't wants in these areas to help you become more clear and focused and begin setting goals and intentions to manifesting what you want.

Wants and Don't Wants (based on a process from The Law of Attraction by Michael Losier)

On a piece of paper, make two columns and write the words "I Don't Want" on the left side, and the words "I Want" on the right column. Now list all of the things you don't like about a specific situation that you are in (from one of the four areas of your life) on the "I Don't Want" side. Once finished, read each line and ask yourself, "What do I want instead?" Cross off the left line and write these answers on the "I Want" side. This very simple exercise helps you really identify what you want and helps you set your intention for how you want to move on with your goals. In the table below is an example of what your "wants" and "don't wants" lists could look like if you were discussing relationships or career.

I Don't Want	I Want
I don't know how to be alone.	I want to feel empowered and excited for my new journey.
I don't want to be home all the time.	I want to fill up my calendar with fun dates with my friends and family.
I am afraid to try things on my own.	I want to enjoy being adventurous and trying all kinds of new activities.

Or if you are choosing career as your topic:

I don't want long hours.	I want to make my own flexible hours.
I don't want to make a small paycheck.	I want to be financially abundant and have enough money to travel and splurge on myself once in a while.
I don't want a boring job.	I want a fulfilling career that makes me feel passionate and excited to go to work.

Once you are done with this list, go down each line on your "want" column and ask yourself, How do I want to feel? Make a note of these as well.

Follow your completed list with a positive affirmation statement that combines your wants into one paragraph. For example, using the first example, from a relationship perspective, it would be something like:

I feel so excited and empowered on my new journey. I fill up my calendar with fun dates with friends and family while having downtime to nurture myself. I enjoy being so adventurous and trying all kinds of new and exciting activities that keep me on my toes. Make sure that you do one subject at a time. The idea is to express and bring out your desires in a juicy and exciting way. This will raise your vibrations, and keep you on a positive note, which will subconsciously begin turning the wheels in your mind to begin aligning you to your desires. When you are finished, print it and keep it on your nightstand or wherever you will see it and can read it daily.

Altruism

While I was in the midst of my divorce, my dearest friend, Carol, suggested I think about getting involved in a charity as a way of taking the focus off my pain and giving back. I immediately joined Heifer International, an organization that fights poverty and hunger in many countries around the world, and I felt a sense of hope and compassion come over me. I joined other charities and became involved in other groups that gave back to the world, such as clean-up groups, hunger and disease walks, and similar. It has become part of my life since then, and I have the deepest respect and admiration for these groups and charities.

If you are where I was and don't have any disposable income to contribute, you can sell your items or collect from family and friends, or if those seem like too much, you can contribute with a little bit of time. You can go to your local soup kitchen, plant a tree, or read a book to children at one of the local schools in your area. There are so many ways you can contribute without money. Being part of one of these charities or events helps shift the focus off you and onto others who desperately need your help. Through your altruistic acts, you release stress, feel stronger, and have a sense of a much deeper purpose. According to Harvard University studies, "There is evidence that altruistic love may activate certain aspects of the relaxation response" and have a lot of other benefits.

The "Is" Box

Now that you are more excited and hopeful about your future, it's time to get an "Is" box. Unlike a "hope chest" where young ladies kept things in anticipation of marriage, an "Is" box is a beautiful box where you will put all of your dreams and things you are going to manifest. It can be things about love or career or anything that makes you smile and makes you feel joy when you think about it. It can be a box you already have, or you can pick one up at your local home store. Make sure it feels special to you.

Inside this box you are going to put intentions, goals, notes, cutout pictures from magazines and photos, and essentially everything you dream and that you are intending on manifesting will go inside this box. Dream big!! Every time you put something inside, you will say "It is." I love to look inside my box at the collections of pictures, notes that I wrote to myself, and goals that I have set for myself. It is really amazing how pretty much everything that I put inside my box has already manifested or is in the process of manifesting. So, every time I put something new inside my box I get really excited because I know it's on its way. It's kind of like a really special vision board or another fun Law of Attraction tool. Give it a try. It's really fun!

Tap into Your Spirituality

Whatever you have as a spiritual practice or religion, or if you don't have any, this is a good time to get curious or really dive into it. Go deeper into meditation, yoga, and reading books about them so that you can reach your highest self. Because you are so much more open-minded now and in a place of empathy and compassion, you will take this in so much more easily and absorb all of the qualities and teachings that they offer. Once I started to open myself to new experiences and really dive into my spirituality, I found that I have been able to uncover so many more layers of myself and have such a deep love for myself and reverence for the world that I have never experienced before.

The first self-help book I read, The Seat of the Soul by Gary Zukav, blew me away and left me completely hooked on wanting to learn more. I was really blessed to have an amazing friend who always pointed me in the right direction and downloaded books and shared his spiritual and meditation practices with me. Nowadays, all you have to do is go online or find meetups to gather this information if you need it. There is so much opportunity for spiritual enrichment now because there is so much access to so many amazing books and so much wonderful information. Take advantage of it and start practicing.

Travel Somewhere New

If it's possible, book that trip to Paris you have always dreamed about or check out that new state park or those trails in your state. Even if it's just to another state or another park, traveling to a new place can be like an amazing and brief start over for your brain. Imagine stepping off an airplane into new surroundings, new cultures, new foods, new music, and new customs. This is exciting on its own but traveling to a new place also helps broaden your perspective, open your mind, and get you a real-life education perfect for your new life chapter. It is something you can keep forever in your memories.

If you can't leave the country just yet, you can still create a lifetime of memories and amazing experiences by visiting new places within your reach. Get out there and visit a new park, a new beach, or another state. The point is to go somewhere new once a year, if possible.

Chapter 14
How to Keep Your Self-Esteem Steady

Even though I am stubborn and fiery by nature, I struggled with the "disease to please others" most of my life. This came from a need to be liked and accepted even at my own expense. It was part socialization, part personality, and part coping mechanism. But it backfired, again and again, causing frustration and resentment. This reflex to ignore my true desires, needs, and even God's voice clouded my judgment. I often said "Yes" when I knew in my heart that "No" was the right answer.

My journey of self-love and self-acceptance intertwines with my faith as well as a steep learning curve with setting boundaries—learning to love myself enough to say no, stick with it, and believe that I'm worth it.

I am not ashamed of all the self-affirmations posted on my mirror and all the prayer slips in my wallet and purse. I need daily reminders that I am loved by God.

If you don't prioritize your physical, mental, and spiritual health, you'll be lucky if someone stops you.

I remember my first boss calling me out when I was working through lunch. "Stop that right now!" Terrified by her authority, my stomach sunk as I thought that I was in trouble.

She met my eyes and calmly stated, "You don't get paid for lunch. So, take it." I sat in silence. "Get the hell out of here because this work will eat you up. Bye!"

She turned abruptly and whisked away onto the elevator. I quickly followed with my half-eaten sandwich. I never stopped taking a lunch break from then on. I would go outside, sit in the nearby courtyard, people watch, and sit in silence.

Taking lunch was actually a big deal. It was my first brush with self-care, and I'm grateful to that boss for teaching it to me. Often, if we don't make our health a priority, no one will stop us. And our jobs will take and take and spit us out if we let them.

American culture prides itself on being busy—always on the go, working hard at the cost of one's health, family time, sleep, face-to-face conversations, and sanity. Ask people in your life, "How are you?" At least in Silicon Valley, the most common response is, "Oh, my gosh. I am so busy." Where does self-care come into play if we barely sleep or eat?

Even as children, we are endlessly pressured to prove ourselves: get good grades, excel in sports, get accepted into a good college, nail a great job. As adults we're expected to make the most of that "great job" and then move up from position to position, no matter the personal cost. It's a never-ending trap.

When did saying "No" begin to feel like a crime? It's actually a healthy behavior and keeps relationships intact. Learning to say "No" is also key to having healthy boundaries. If we are overscheduled, overworked, and overstressed, it is even more vital that we can draw a line in the sand at times and say "No" to take care of ourselves, succeed at what we really want to do or just recuperate from life.

When do we value ourselves for being human in the midst of our failures and brokenness? When do we go beyond the to-do list and look at whether we are really fulfilled in our lives? When do we sit in silence or just do nothing?

Give Yourself to God

So many times, it is easier to just get through the day, mindlessly following the daily routine and overscheduling ourselves.

Letting go of control is our biggest fear because there are so many unanswered questions and variables in life. So much of my life has been learning how to surrender and trust the process. God is doing the battling for me, and I really don't have to micromanage his role in my life.

Am I following my gut, God's word? Am I on the right track or am I going nowhere? Am I operating out of ego? So much doubt and self-judgment persist.

Any success by society's standards will give out, expire, or evaporate over time. All things lose their shine, including the optimal circumstances. We need something more in life and something more to ground our marriage throughout our lives.

We are living in a temporal time and our lives belong to God. He chooses when we go, how we go. Our challenge is to be here now, make something of our lives, and find meaning in the midst of the hot mess.

Getting ready for marriage is committing to a partner who gets that the game is rigged against you in the material world, that basing a union on faith is the closest way to building a foundation from rock—God being the only constant you can count on.

Real life will break you down. Failure is inevitable and happens every day. The only way to love yourself is to embrace your heart and have the strength to not buckle to the pressures of the outside world.

Don't give your power to anyone or anything to complete you—just give your relationship up to God. This is the best start for any partnership.

God is your ally, your truth-teller, and your secret sauce when the material world tells you lies. Your faith is your backbone when the world won't let up and you can't look up or stand up. When you identify with the world, you take on its endless suffering, misery, injustice, and pain. When you hold onto God, you live by what really matters the most.

When you go to your spiritual source, God shows you that there is a bigger picture, more meaning than meets the eye, and that who you are is not determined by your environment. Don't buy that story. You are not my social media handle; You are bigger than that.

Internalizing your self-worth and value can seriously rock your world, including your most intimate relationships. God calls us to Him in self-forgiveness and self-acceptance.

As you accept yourself and become aware of your needs, you learn to discern what is right for you, which is not based on what you were taught or shown as a child. This may mean challenging childhood traditions or norms—what has been expected of you for years, if not generations.

Chapter 15
How to Feel Alive Again

Acceptance

If you're reading this and are committed to making your relationship work, I am certain that you will find acceptance. It's the people slashing tires that I wonder about. As for you, I know that you will eventually come to a point of acceptance if you focus on healing the pain and dealing with your emotions.

- I say that because if you're so interested in finding ways to cope with and heal from this act of infidelity, then you are the type of person that will find healthy ways to heal. You're doing it right now, and you will find acceptance as long as you take some of the advice you find here (and maybe some other helpful advice you find elsewhere).
- Keep in mind that acceptance doesn't mean that you are 100% okay with what occurred. It simply means that you found a new normal for your new reality. The new reality can be tolerable for you, or you may explore ways to make your new normal better than your old normal. Regardless, you have to accept that normal will be different now. If you keep fighting to get back to old normal, you're fighting an impossible fight. The sooner you realize things are different and

that you are in control of charting out your new normal, the sooner you will find true acceptance.

- You're getting educated on healthy ways to cope, and you're being strong and courageous. To be honest, I'm not too worried about you at all. I know you're on the right path. However, I want to help you heal as quickly as possible. I want you to follow these tips to make sure that you are able to heal properly.

Don't Blame Yourself

The first lesson you need to learn is that you absolutely cannot blame yourself for his actions. The situation has already happened, and it makes no sense to blame yourself. After all, you didn't make him cheat. It wasn't because of something you did wrong. It was a lack of character in him.

Sitting around feeling pity, disgust or guilt won't change the past and they are not healthy emotions for you to focus on. Your man made a selfish decision and in no way does his selfishness represent your self-worth. You are absolutely not to blame for his actions. He created this problem, not you, so stop the blame game!

You Are Stronger Than Your Pain

Yes, the pain hurts, and yes, your pain is very real, but the good news is that your pain won't last forever. Whenever we tend to be down in the dumps, we think the dumps will be the new normal and that things will never change. But this is the wrong mindset. Things will change and they will get better—in time.

In order to get over something as serious as infidelity, you will have to be super strong. I mean Wonder Woman strong. You have to be strong, courageous, open-minded and resilient.

You will have to be strong because if you're not, you will fall victim to guilt and sorrow. As stated—it's not your fault! Having said that, being strong sometimes means feeling even those deeper emotions of sadness and loss.

It's perfectly normal to feel pain and sadness because a form of trust has been violated within your relationship. You can't avoid these feelings. Your goal is to find strength from these negative feelings; you could even say your goal is to come out stronger in the end.

And yes, there will be an end to these negative feelings. It could be days, weeks, months or maybe even years—but it will happen. The timeframe is not really important. What is important is that you find ways to cope and heal in a healthy way. What you should do is focus on the sadness and pain. You don't want to drink, do drugs or wallow in self-pity listening to slow songs and crying your eyes out. That's simply not helpful.

Instead, you want to feel the pain by giving yourself a set time each day to feel it and then move to a position of strength.

Being Strong

Right now, you're probably not feeling very strong. Truth be told, you probably feel very weak. Well, the good news is that you are not weak! You are a warrior.

To see yourself as the strong woman you are, I want you to picture yourself in a boxing match. I really mean this…I want you to form a strong mental picture right now. Visualize another woman trying to knock out your spirit. Yes, your opponent is tough, but so are you. In her neck of the woods, she's known as the hardest hitter in the sport. They call her Heartbreak. You are named Resilient. Let's see what happens.

Well, Heartbreak has just hit you with a crippling body blow, a punch to the gut so hard you swear it knocked your soul straight out of your back. Down to the mat you go, and there you lie while the referee counts. 1, 2, 3, 4…

Now, it would be really easy to lie there, let the referee count to ten, and let Heartbreak win. In no time at all, the paramedics and trainers would rush into the ring to tend to you. They help you walk and then fill you with positive words of encouragement about how she was no match for you. They may even tell you that you were robbed or hit with a low blow. Although this might make you feel better temporarily, you would still feel defeated, angry and frustrated that you didn't crush Heartbreak and leave her wincing in pain. After all, they call you Resilient for a reason. You could have taken her on.

So, you decide to get up because you're called Resilient for a reason. You decide to fight back and reclaim your dignity and your strength. You decide to pick yourself up, regain your stamina and fight back with everything you've got.

The ref counts…five, six, seven. You muster all your life's energy and strength to get to one knee. Eight. Now you feel stronger and are standing tall.

Nine. You stand up, right before the ref counts to ten. You decide that you're going to keep fighting for what yourself and then you deliver a knockout punch to Heartbreak. You knock her out cold and she doesn't get back up.

Instead of feeling weak, you now feel strong and courageous. You feel empowered and ready to deal with whatever is thrown your way next. You have decided that you're not finished yet! You want to win and save your relationship. You can do this, but you've got to be strong enough to fight for your relationship.

Other women, just like you, have done it. Women who were Wonder Woman strong women, who have been knocked down, face flat on the mat, and out for the count too. Like you, they chose to get up. They chose not to give up. You are just like them. You are Wonder Woman strong, and because of that you will come out of this situation a better person.

Being Courageous

But what's courage got to do with it? Everything!

First, it takes courage to throw caution to the wind and give him another chance. People may try and talk you out of it. They may not understand why you want to stay with him. They may even tell you that you'll never be able to trust him again. They may tell you that you're being naïve and stupid. I say f*ck them.

You know your man and your relationship better than anyone else. No one has a right to judge you for giving him another chance. Those same people judging you from an outside perspective may think they know best, but they don't. You know what's best. You know what makes you happy and what makes you sad. You know if being with him is better than being without him.

Trust yourself and ignore well-meaning friends and family members who want you to cut him loose. Thank them for their interest but tell them to mind their own damn business. Seriously, though, tell them that you appreciate their concern, but you are going to manage your relationship in a way that you think is best.

Let them know that you appreciate and love them, but you have decided to do what's best for you—and that is to work things out.

Being Open-Minded

No one should ever cheat when they're involved in a monogamous and committed relationship, but many people do so. In fact, studies have been done that show that cheating is the norm for many people. (Not that I'm condoning cheating, but I just want you to see that you are not alone). Many women, just like you, have gone through this.

Whatever reaction you have is a reasonable response but remember to stay open-minded and focused on your comfort. Only you and your man can determine the best way to overcome the situation and find a path towards healing. The most important part of your reaction is that you make these decisions together.

Being Resilient

As we conversed earlier, your nickname is Resilient. You are called that for a reason.

This is how I want you to be: resilient. I want you to be able to return to your original self, content in your relationship despite being put through the ringer. Resiliency in life is important because life isn't always fair. You will consistently be challenged, and so being able to remain flexible will help you deal with all of life's twists and turns. The majority of your life's challenges will be because of your relationships with others, and right now you face the mother of all challenges: infidelity.

Before we talk about ways to make you more resilient, first, I must commend you. You already have proven to be somewhat resilient. I mean, you could have taken the easy way out of this predicament and just ended the relationship; after all, that is what society expected of you. But no, you decided to go against the societal grain and fight for what you believe in—in this case, your relationship.

Chapter 16
How to Deal With New Relationships after Suffering a Betrayal

Giving Marriage another Chance

Just because your wife cheated on you doesn't necessarily mean that all women are likely to cheat on you. It doesn't also mean the end of marrying.

Going for a second marriage is like repeating a class. Repeating lessons. However, you never get the same grades. You've got a greater potential to score higher, since, in addition you also have the experience to cap it. While it may seem tedious to revise your notes on marriage, it is the best thing to do if you want to improve your chances and performance this time around. Here, were are simply revising most of what you already know, or ought to know. It is good not to assume, just as you can't assume an exam by not revising.

Give a Chance

After dating, and after thoroughly exposing yourself to different suitors, one will come out above the rest. That is the one meant for you.

If you feel you have the gusto to settle down, yes, give her a chance. There is nothing wrong trying. You never get the best until you keep on trying.

Establish a Strong Marriage Foundation

Every builder knows that a house established on quicksand never lasts. A weak foundation is the primary cause of sinking houses and a myriad of cracks. Your marriage is such kind of a house that you must ensure that it doesn't sink because of

a weak foundation.

You are already a builder – having built your first marriage. However, that doesn't necessarily mean that you know it all. It also doesn't mean that you have not forgotten how to handle some of the tools, and how to employ some of the techniques. The technology could have brought new tools and new techniques. Why employ the obsolete? And can obsolete tools and techniques work when you are trying to build a modern house? Maybe not. In simple terms, you have to re-learn. A second marriage is unlike the first one. Yet, this is a new opportunity to avoid the blunders and seal the loopholes that made the first 'house' leak.

Not bad to revisit. Not bad to revise. There is nothing wrong with repeating lessons, but there is everything wrong with failing to learn.

To establish a strong foundation for a house, the following are key considerations a builder makes;

- Expert knowledge of construction
- Quality of material ingredients to be used
- A proper mix ratio of the various key material ingredients

- The kind of ground upon which the foundation is established

You are the builder of your own marriage and family. This is heavily mirrored in the key considerations to factor in making a solid beginning in marriage.

Making a Solid Beginning

Just as in establishing a house foundation, to make a solid beginning in marriage, you need to consider:

- Your own expertise in gauging the kind of marriage ingredients need for an enduring, lasting and happy marriage.

- The quality of your relationship (which happens to be the primary material in marriage).

- The proper mix ratio of the various traits (character and personality compatibility) required for the kind of marriage that you deserve.

- The kind of background you are in vis-à-vis that of your potential marriage partner as forming the basis for your marriage.

Your own expertise: gaining knowledge about what marriage is all about

Most people enter into marriage without sufficient knowledge of what it entails. Having been married before, you are a lot more knowledgeable than those who are in the process of marrying for the first time.

Nonetheless, when the first marriage fails, it means that you are starting all over again... except that you have abundant experience and a lot of knowledge. It would be ignorant for us to assume that we know what you don't or do. However, for the sake of those who may be lacking, or simply want to refresh their knowledge.

Should you need to up your knowledge, the following are some of the important sources from which you can easily get requisite information on matters relating to marriage;

- Your very own family
- Your local religious institution
- Marriage seminars
- Marriage counselors
- Trusted couples that you are close to
- The quality of your relationship

Sometimes you need to gauge the quality of your relationship to determine its fitness for purpose – marriage. More often than not, many people mistake the romantic relationship as automatically leading to marriage. This romance is definitely an important ingredient for a relationship, but it cannot stand on its own.

The following are quality factors to consider in determining as to whether your existing relationship can lead to marriage or not;

- Love – love is not romance, love is not attraction, love is not lust. Love is an affection that is filled with compassion and endures all challenges against it.

- Friendship -friendship is love and beyond. It is love actualized into a workable partnership.

- Shared values – there ought to be compatibility in values. When there lacks compatibility in the most basic and most important of your values, then, marriage will be weak and won't withstand tremors and quakes of life.

- Shared goals – shared goals bring forth a shared destiny in marriage. Without shared goals, marriage crumbles due to each partner pursuing a parallel and often contradictory direction.

- Strength of character – compassion, uprightness, discipline, honesty, commitment, forthrightness, empathy, respect, patience, understanding, among others, should manifest in you and your partner.

The mix ratio of various key attributes

Both parties to the marriage have unique traits and attributes. No one can be absolute in everything. Even if you share the same values, they are never going to be exact or in equal measure. Just like any material, it has various elements that comprise it. The mix ratio of these elements greatly determines its quality. This is the same for partners who intent upon getting married to each other.

Some of these key attributes include:

- Virtues - compassion, uprightness, discipline, honesty, commitment, forthrightness, empathy, respect, patience, understanding, resilience, assertiveness, trust, among others.

- Good habits – greetings, charming groom, hygiene, good communication etiquette, healthy sleep-wake habits, among others.

- Positive attitude – the inspiring outlook of life – especially the family relationship, go-getter attitude, cheerfulness and entertaining, among others

You have to consider which of these key attributes are much more required for the kind of your marriage than others. Prioritize them based on the order of importance. Check whether those of your partner and your own do correlate (not necessarily matching absolutely) and whether they complement and or supplement each other. If there is no correlation, complementation or supplementation to what you are looking for, then, it is easy for incompatibilities to set in. Incompatibility is one of the leading causes of separation and divorce.

Give a Compassionate Thought to the Likely Beneficiaries of Your New Marriage

Most marriages are intended to result in a family with at least one child. Many partners don't give forethought about a child they intend to have thus leaving matters to fate. However, with modern-day challenges of bringing up a child into a productive adult, it is no longer a matter of leaving everything pertaining to a child's future to fate. Partners have to be actively involved in planning for their potential child's future.

Some of the most important concerns about a potential child that couples need to consider include;

- Establishing a conducive environment for having a child – a child should have a safe and loving environment. A child should feel wanted and loved by both parents. A quarrelsome environment where parents clash most of the time is such a strenuous environment for a child.

- Establishing the standard of living expected of your child – plan for your child. It is no longer an act of animalistic instinct in having a child. A child needs some standard of living that can afford him/her a decent and fair opportunity at life such as good education, good health, and a friendly environment.

- Establishing the kind of values, you expect to impart to your child – a child's success in the future depends so much on enduring values imparted into him/her. It is much more important than material provision. Values such as honesty, tolerance, compassion, respect, discipline, among other virtues are much important than any material wealth you can bequeath your child. This is guaranteed to last but material possessions are not.

Live your lives as parents in such a way that they become a living testimony of how your child ought to live. A child learns more from practical examples than mere words of advice.

Children emulate their parents more than anyone else. So, don't take it for granted.

Chapter 17
Why Not Seek Revenge?

If you are open to contemplating forgiveness but find your mind pulling you toward fantasies or plans of revenge...that's okay, relax—you're only human. Thoughts of revenge can be considered a natural state of mind. In my therapeutic experiences, many people find themselves exploring fantasies of revenge upon which they will never act. Michael E. McCullough, a University of Miami professor, argues that the revenge response is evolutionary, suggesting that it kept early humans safe by deterring would-be enemies from harming them. What's more, it may actually make you feel better in the moment, as simply fantasizing about revenge for an extended period activates the dorsal striatum in the brain, the same part stimulated by sex and chocolate. When economists from the University of Zurich uncovered this in 2004, they proposed that this kick in our brain incentivizes us to seek revenge, even if the ultimate cost comes at our own expense much like eating too much chocolate might. That is an important factor to consider. The drive you feel toward revenge is a product of chemical releases in your brain, which brings you a temporary feeling of relief from your pain. It is important that you pull back for a moment and consider the long-term ramifications of your actions. Revenge may give you temporary relief from your pain now, but it will not leave you feeling better in the long run.

While revenge certainly is an option, the question is whether it will ultimately serve you, your health, your spouse, your divorce outcome, or if applicable, your children. Studies suggest it will not revenge, maintained as a passing thought rather than an obsessive one, and may serve as a supportive coping behavior by offering temporary relief. However, the act of "getting even" with your estranged partner ultimately perpetuates your experience of negative emotions, like anger, guilt, and shame, and may leave you holding greater negative energy than you had prior to acting on the revenge. If you feel your desire for revenge is impeding your ability to move forward toward forgiveness, you might consider taking a moment to utilize the revenge fantasy exercise for forgiveness to assist you in moving along in your emotional processing and toward your post-divorce vision.

Self-Awareness Requires Courage

I have had countless clients assert their willingness to forgive only if the other person was willing to apologize first. If you feel you are willing to forgive but only if your estranged partner apologizes, you might be allowing your path to freedom to be interrupted by your partner's lack of self-awareness. Your ex may have limited recognition or understanding of how they have wronged you; they may have what is referred to in psychotherapy as "low ego strength." Ego strength accounts for our resilience in difficult situations, and those with higher ego strength tend to have higher emotional intelligence. Emotional intelligence, a term made popular by researcher Daniel Goleman, can be understood as one's capacity to manage one's own emotions, as well as the emotions of others. If your partner lacks the insight to examine the ways their behavior has hurt you—they likely have a low EQ capacity. Or, they may simply lack the courage to face the negative feelings within themselves and those which they have caused you by their behavior. If your ex lacks the courage necessary for self-awareness, do not let this deter or block your progress toward your post-divorce vision!

Owning mistakes is more difficult for some than others. You may know (or have married) someone who struggles to say "I'm sorry" regardless of how obvious their culpability seems. These people, in my experience, are those that feel overloaded with shame when owning fault in a situation, and thus, avoid their responsibility to make amends. To be clear, we all make mistakes and hurt others, knowingly and unknowingly. You and your partner are no exception. But ultimately, what you may be holding on to is really disappointment about what they lack in ego strength or courage. It may be their inability to fully acknowledge that they've hurt you that fuels your anger, rather than the behaviors or events they have perpetrated against you (albeit those were likely wrong as well).

It is my suspicion that if you reflect back on your relationship, your partner's frustrating personality was present throughout your marriage. You may now be struggling with the reality of who you selected as your life partner and how they operate in the world. Rather than some particular bad behavior that hurt or disrespected you, you may now be realizing you compromised yourself for your relationship in ways you wished you hadn't. You might even find that deep beneath your disappointment with your partner is anger with yourself for not knowing how their unfavorable character traits would ultimately hurt you. Perhaps, you are angry with yourself for not handling things differently to protect yourself. Your work in this case is to be honest about who you picked as a life partner. In some way, for some reason, this person appeared to fit you at the time of your decision. Typically, this is because there was some way you needed to grow—something you needed to learn about yourself from the relationship. Learn to accept that this person is who you chose to marry and accept their limitations as part of their humanness. Let go of expecting something other than who they are and what they can realistically give you at this time. This is not the same thing as learning to like who they are or how they behave, but only to accept it and stop hoping in vain for a different response during marriage, divorce, or beyond.

Something to consider we often attribute to others the perspectives that we ourselves possess, assuming others must also have our same awareness and abilities. But I can tell you firsthand, as a psychologist that everyone's brain operates differently. The skills you have personally developed and the way you perceive situations may not align with how others function and see things, particularly, in this case, your ex. The fact is, your ex may not be willing or able, at this time, to recognize and address the issues you would like them to address. In lieu of their courage to change, you can still choose to show up as a Heart Warrior—to detach from them with love and free yourself from the bondage of your anger. The choice to find that freedom is yours alone. You can do this through forgiveness.

Chapter 18
What To Do If You Were Forced To Leave

Divorce always involves sin.

Now before you dismiss what I'm saying, I do not believe that everyone who is divorced is guilty of sin. Just like a crime victim is not guilty of the crime, if you were an unwilling participant in the divorce and did nothing to give your spouse biblical grounds for divorce, I believe that the Bible is clear that you are not guilty of sin for the divorce. The spouse who caused the divorce is guilty of breaking his vow to God. Period. In some cases, both spouses may be guilty of sin in God's eyes for the divorce, but in most cases, only one spouse has acted in a way that breaks the marriage covenant.

This has very little relationship to which spouse actually files for divorce. In many instances, the spouse who ultimately files for divorce is not the one who broke the marriage vows. The vows were broken by the sinful acts of the other spouse. The one who is forced to file for divorce is just legally documenting the reality of their broken marriage.

So, to sum up my views of divorce, I believe that in most cases there is a guilty party and an innocent party--one spouse for whom the divorce is a sin and must be repented, and one party who is largely the victim of the other's sin. The innocent party is free in God's eyes.

If you were the one who was forced to leave, now what? How do you go on?

While I don't have direct experience with this, my current wife was in a situation where she had no choice but to leave her marriage, so I asked her what that felt like. The feelings she had during that time were not that different from what I experienced: anger, betrayal, fear, loss of control, bitterness, relief. She described the same basic feelings anyone who is going through a divorce feels, but from a different perspective than mine.

So, if you were forced to divorce your ex because of infidelity, abuse, addictions, abandonment, etc., I will try to offer some advice on how to cope and how to move on.

Take Ownership

Like I've said before, a key part in the healing process is to take ownership of your part in the breakdown of your marriage. We all share some responsibility for our failed marriages. It may be neglect of the marriage, putting kids before your spouse, spending too much time at work, or it may simply be that you made an extremely poor choice for a life partner. Whatever your role, taking ownership of it will help you move through the healing process, and will also help you be better prepared for future relationships.

Don't Blame Yourself

So just after getting on a soapbox about taking ownership, now I'm going to tell you not to blame yourself. You cannot control what another person does. Even though you share some responsibility for the breakdown of the marriage, the fact that your ex chose to break her marriage vows is not your fault.

No marriage is perfect. If your ex was unhappy in some way, then the right thing to do was to try to fix the problem. But unfortunately, it takes two willing people to make a marriage work. Many are just not willing to do the hard work required to have a good relationship.

My ex refused to go to counseling both during the marriage when things were definitely salvageable and during the divorce process. She had a long list of complaints about me and our marriage but was unwilling to work on it. Having been raised in a religious tradition that looked down on divorced people, I went through a period of self-blame. Ultimately I came to the realization that I didn't want the divorce but couldn't make her stay, so how could it be my fault? I didn't do anything that would have been biblical grounds for divorce, so my conscience is clear.

Forgive

Forgiving my ex is the single thing that did the most to move me along in the healing process. It took quite a while but releasing her into God's hands finally gave me peace to move on. Forgiving doesn't mean that what your ex did was OK or that you are willing to take him back. It simply means that you are not going to hold it against him or allow what he did to have a hold on you.

Don't Be a Woman/Man Hater

The pain of divorce is so difficult, especially if you were emotionally or physically abused, or your spouse was unfaithful to you, that it can be easy to assume that all women or all men are just like your ex.

They're not!

Dating too quickly is one of the biggest mistakes people make in the divorce process. I would never pressure someone to date if they are not ready, but mistrust of the opposite sex can go way beyond a reluctance to date and spill over into other personal and professional relationships. If you find yourself being a hater, step back and analyze your feelings. You'll find that they are not rational.

You may be hurt so badly that you can't imagine ever wanting to be in another relationship and that's fine. But if you find it moving to "hater" status then you need to take a step back and try to understand why you are feeling that way. A pastor or counselor can help you work through your problems with the opposite sex.

Chapter 19
Healing

Nine times out of ten the one that committed a major offence in a relationship, marriage, a friendship, or life in general will be looking for forgiveness as soon as possible. It's not just the major offender but its people in general that are consistently looking for forgiveness, Grace, and Mercy for themselves when they offend others. But how many of those same offenders are willing to give forgiveness, Grace, and Mercy when they are offended? Well that is another million-dollar question that I do not have the answer to. Regarding infidelity or a major offence, the offence is not just damaging to the spouse that has been offended but it typically is very hurtful and damaging to the person that actually committed the infidelity or a major offence. During an affair there can be an internal moral struggle, and, in many cases, people have adapted quite well to living a double life until that double life comes to a crashing end.

Why the heart ache when the affair comes to a crashing end. I cannot say for all but for me and what I have learned from speaking to many others that have had affairs. Is when the affair is taking place there is an unknown factor that exists. We may be hurting our spouse by our words, actions, lack of intimacy and so forth but the real pain of an infidelity never truly hits until the offender confess his or her unloyalty. We can be like inspector clue-so gathering concrete information daily but if our spouse denies his or her actions even if caught read handed with their hand in the pot it still does not burn the same. It sometimes does not hit home until we hear the words come out of their mouth. Yes, I have been unfaithful, I had, or I am having an affair. At that point that is when our blood starts pumping and our heart starts pounding so hard, we have to hold our chest or precisely gasp for each breath taken. The pain truly sets into the heart, body mind and soul from the pain delivered to us from the one that should have protected us. As our loved one express anger, pain, words of expressing humiliation, suicidal thoughts, uncontrollable tears, hysterical crying episodes now the offender sees firsthand the destruction that he or she has caused. An affair does not mean that that person committing the wrongful act does not genuinely love their spouse. It typically means that there is a severe underlying issue or issues that are not being addressed in the marriage, within the person committing the offence or even within the person that the offence was committed against.

Our Councilor and founder of Couples Academy, Hasani Pettiford explained to my wife and I that people do not get divorced over infidelity they get divorced over what caused the infidelity. Furthermore, he explained that the infidelity exposes that there is an underlying issue like one of the three I just stated. I don't know about you but that was a huge eye opener for me and my wife. But I have also learned that people not only get divorced over the root issue that sparked the infidelity, but another huge reason is how the spouse or offender shows up after the infidelity is discovered. If he or she acts as if it's no big deal with a; just get over it type of attitude more than likely in due time divorce will follow during the discovery period or sometime after.

Now that the affair has been exposed and admitted to. The bleeding starts and the offender stand helpless before the spouse and cannot stop the bleeding. A person placed in this predicament even if he or she is the blame for their own actions you have to be absolutely cold hearted, cold blooded and absolutely self-centered not to have any remorse for your actions. If you are not any of the types that I mentioned this is where the damage of our own actions starts to affect (our self) the offender. I know no one that is devastated having their dreams of a beautiful marriage and life crushed before their very eyes by the one they loved and trusted in wants to hear that the guilty offender is hurting but it very well may be the truth and regardless like it or not this is what commonly takes place.

Truth be told if you have the slightest bit of wanting to restore and save your marriage this is the type of person you want standing before you. I am not saying that they will not come with their own set of challenges to overcome because self-condemnation can be a heart wrenching devastating issue to overcome but for sure I would prefer someone that has to find forgiveness of them self than a careless, cold hearted life sucking woman standing before me that does not give a dam about me or her actions. As a man, just imagine your wife telling you it happened just get over it! I ask to imagine because I have heard of many men telling their wives just get over it because they are not in an affair anymore. I have heard that statement more so from men but have also heard it from woman but either way it's a potential relationship burial statement! If my wife told me that I would have called the police on myself to save myself from myself. With all of our wrongful actions I have never had the audacity to tell my wife get over it! Married 32 almost 33 years we have had a few heated fellowships (Arguments) LOL but I never raised my hand to strike my wife. But with that kind of disrespect and lack of remorse I think that would be the straw that breaks the camel's back. I think as I call the police on myself, I would have to flee our home at the same time to again save myself from myself LOL.

Chapter 20
The Most Powerful Creatures on the Planet

I believe that women are the most powerful creatures on the planet. We create life in our bodies. Think about that. We literally have the ability to make life inside of us. Sure, not all by ourselves, but after that initial part, yes, we very much do the heavy lifting. And after we create it, we birth it, keep it alive, and nurture it, all while balancing 1,000 other things. This is incredible. We are strong, we are emotional, we are brilliant, and we are capable of more than we give ourselves credit for. I truly believe that women need to come together more and realize how brilliant we are. That we don't need to tear each other down out of fear that we aren't good enough or won't have what what's her name has. We are unlimited and boundless beings that can-do incredible things.

I want any woman where I was, to know that she is capable of anything that she wants. We were not created or put on this earth to just eat shit all the time and live on other people's terms. We are put here to create the life that we want and desire. Unfortunately, we don't get what we deserve; we get what we believe deep down on the inside to be true.

You must stop being so afraid to color outside the lines. Stop being afraid to take chances. Start listening to that voice inside of you that tells you what your real desires are and go for them. NOW. The only boundaries of what we can have and create are the ones that we put on ourselves. You know that girl you follow on social media, the one that travels all the time with unlimited amounts of money, wearing the best clothes who seems to have zero problems in life? First, she probably does have a shit load of problems (they just aren't as fun to post, imagine #crying selfie—not so cute). Second, she probably pisses you off. She probably pisses you off, because you don't think that is possible for you. BUT IT IS. Your triggers all exist to show you what you are avoiding, or what you want to be more like. They are all telling you something. They aren't bothersome, random things that occur just to piss you off. They are KNOWLEDGE that you can use to make changes to yourself (and therefor change your reality).

Don't be afraid to try to go for your dreams and fail. My entire life, I wanted to be a published author and write a book. I could never figure out what to write about. Through one of the worst situations and my biggest failures to date, this guidebook you are holding in your hands was born. On the other side of my biggest mistakes and lessons were some of my biggest dreams. When I prayed that night in the bathroom that God and the Universe would take from me that which no longer served me, I knew that changes would come. I let it go. Less than a month after, my ex was ripped from me and my old life burned down with it. Ask and you shall receive.

I never would have become all that I am or do the things that I wanted to do, if that situation stayed the same. I don't want you to go through the hell, and all of the pain or the suffering that I went through—I don't wish that upon anyone—but I want you to realize what you are worth. Wake up to the fact that you are worthy and capable of accomplishing your desires. Stop being afraid to go for your dreams and stop letting excuses get in the way. The only thing in your way is your own mind. Feed your mind goodness. If you need some other incredible books (besides this one of course) to help you on your journey.

I have so many incredible women in my life that I see holding themselves back, because of what they believe or what society tells them to be true. I knew someone with a little baby who desperately didn't want to be with the father anymore but felt that if she broke up with him that no one would want to date her because she has a baby. Are you telling me that there wasn't a man out there who would cherish the incredible fucking gifts of human beings she and her child are? That he wouldn't thank the lucky stars every night that they were both created? Because, there was a man out there who would feel that way. The only thing holding her back from the happiness that she knew in heart she deserved was HERSELF.

Sure, walking away from a relationship when you have a child is frightening. It's hard. It's not just you that you have to think about anymore. However, the relationship has served its purpose, and, in this case, it has very much run its course. In her case, I believed everything she was waiting for was on the other side of it. And, no, I am not encouraging all women with kids to break up with their spouses. I am talking about a very specific scenario here. Obviously, when families stay together and can be happy, that is ideal. However, this was not the case here. And, guess what? This girl walked away from that relationship and did indeed meet the man of her dreams. It happened fast and it happened easily. What if she had never had the lady balls to do it? She'd probably still be sitting unhappily next to a man who didn't love her enough to work on their relationship and be the spouse she truly deserved, allowing her to be the woman she desperately knew she could be. She'd be teaching her child to settle, to be boxed in, to not go for their dreams. Instead, she gets to teach her child what a loving, happy, healthy relationship looks like every day. Good for her.

If you have wanted to be an author, a teacher, a lawyer, someone who travels for a living, I challenge you to start taking chances. Start taking actions every day toward that goal. You don't have to figure it all out or know exactly how it will happen. You just have to believe that it is possible. Believe in yourself and know that you are worthy of the desires inside of your heart. Your time is incredibly valuable. Stop wasting it on things that don't matter. There are women who make money posting about tea in their underwear on Instagram. There are men who make money playing their favorite sports. There are kids who make money showing off their toys on YouTube. ANYTHING is possible. The Internet has literally taken away the boundaries of space and time. It's no longer difficult to start a business or make connections with those who can assist you in up leveling your life. You have no excuse anymore. You have been given all the tools to become what you desire to be, do, and have.

People telling me I couldn't create a good life by myself infected my way of thinking, and it was a long time before I realized that they couldn't imagine it for themselves, therefore they couldn't imagine it for me. Sometimes, people want to keep you safely in the box that makes sense in their own minds, because they don't think they are capable of things, so why should you be? That would be truly uncomfortable for them. It would challenge everything they believe in and show them that they are missing out on their true potential, and that would be frightening for them. Maybe they are comfortable in their safe little bubble where challenging the status quo is scary.

I am not that person, and if you are holding this guidebook in your hands, I don't think that you are either. Other people's thoughts, comments, and beliefs on YOUR life are only a reflection of THEIRS. It has everything to do with their own thoughts and triggers, of what they believe to be true, and zero to do with what is actually true for you. Most of the time, the people we take advice from don't even have the things we want or live the life that we want. Be careful who you choose to listen to.

There have been so many times in my life that I didn't have a person to look up to. I didn't know many people living life as an entrepreneur. I didn't know many people who had successfully moved away from my small little town. I didn't know many women who made more money than their male counterparts and bought whatever the hell they wanted to because they thought they could. I didn't know many people who ran their own businesses on the Internet. I don't know many people who have written books or become authors. I have had strong, brilliant women around me and in my family for decades, and they have taught me a lot, but I haven't had many examples of people whose life I wanted to emulate.

However, if you wait around for an example of what to do next to get you where you want to go, you may not find one. If you take one thing from this guidebook, it's that you are capable of anything that you want. You deserve to have a fulfilling life and all the crazy, obnoxious, shiny shit that goes with it. The only person standing in your way is the person in the mirror. Invest in yourself and in your mind, and you will be amazed at the places you will go. It is NEVER too late to reinvent yourself. I do it every day. Life can either be a wonderful, brilliant adventure, or it can suck balls. It's up to you, my love.

It's your decision to make.

Chapter 21
Ending the Self-blame, Guilt and Regrets

We all know what it is like to feel bad about something that's happened in our lives, and often no more so than when facing the end of a long-term relationship. Whether initiated or not, whether someone else is involved or not, the loss of our dreams and the fear that we may well have played a part in their demise, as well as anxiety for the unknown future, can be anything from uncomfortable to paralyzing. Feeling guilty and blaming ourselves undermines our self-worth, confidence, and self-esteem. We regret what happened; we wish we'd acted or said things differently. We give ourselves a hard time because we judge ourselves as bad.

For someone to be guilty, there also has to be blame somewhere. In other words, someone has to have been considered to have done something wrong.

So, let's take this step by step.

For example:

Are you not happy about something? Have you done something you feel has caused a problem for someone or created a situation that leaves you feeling guilty and uncomfortable?

If yes, do you feel that you would act differently were you in that situation again?

Can you do something to make amends, if appropriate? Perhaps a sincere verbal or written acceptance of your role in the situation is in order.

If you have done what you can and felt to be your best, has the situation been amended or resolved? If yes, that's great. Now you can let it go. If not, let it go anyway. It's over. If you have done the external action that needed doing, then that's the end of it. Now it's time to let it go internally, to release it from within you and move on.

This level of honesty with yourself will also help you face situations more realistically and help you see what has been happening between you and your ex-partner.

Again, letting go doesn't mean condoning unacceptable behavior in another, but it does involve acknowledgement of the facts of the situation, and also recognizing that the only person you can change is yourself. To try to do anything else will only drive you nuts. You'll have to accept that at some point, so it's a great idea to do it up front. I promise you; there is a huge relief when this happens, huge. It is like having a weight lifted from you.

It's the holding on that gives us pain and causes distress. Some people are so laid back nothing much bothers them; they take life as it comes, are positive in their outlook, and they roll with any blows. How many people do you know who are genuinely laid back and distressed? It's just not possible, is it? So, take a good look at what you are holding onto—and know that this is what is causing you pain in some form or another. When you can recognize this for what it is, let it go, and bring yourself back to the present. You are then on your way to mastering yourself and how you feel no matter what the circumstances.

No more guilt. No more self-blame. You are doing your best, and I want you to know you are not a bad person because your relationship is breaking up. You are moving towards being able to accept the situation as a fact and understand that there are steps you can take to move past the pain.

You possibly want to know how you got to where you are in the first place, and how can you make sure it doesn't happen again.

Here are a few things to look at. See if they resonate with you and the way you feel about yourself.

Why Another Can Never Complete Us

Looking to another to complete you is where there is emotional or psychological reliance on a partner to feel secure, worthy, or fulfilled.

Reliance is often a mutual aspect of an ongoing relationship. For example, you may notice that an outgoing personality will tend to attract a more introverted person, or a scattered person may go for a more steadying partner. A bully will look for a submissive person, and an unsure person may search for strength in another (who then may turn out to be a bully).

There is a tendency to look for another to fill in the gaps where there are feelings, conscious or subconscious, of not being complete or whole, or where there is a feeling that there are some characteristics or features missing or underdeveloped. Someone who perhaps feels disorganized and loses opportunities because of it may well seek a more organized partner. The more organized partner may welcome the greater spontaneity the other shows, perhaps aware that being over organized has its pitfalls by limiting what life can offer in the moment.

In this simple example, while both are happy with this situation, they will get on well. But what tends to happen over time is that the organized person will begin to tire of the unreliability of the more scattered one, and the scattered one starts to resent being organized by another.

As this situation continues, there are three choices.

1. It can get too much, and they will separate, deciding to look for a better match. Though by not addressing the underlying issues, the situation will most likely repeat itself in one form or another.

2. They can try to ride the upsets as they happen and push the issues under the carpet. This denial can seemingly work well for a time. But there will be a build-up of resentment, and, as a result, there will quite probably be times when the situation explodes.

3. The third option is for both partners to look honestly at themselves and where they are seeking completeness in another (and then in turn also resenting it). If both change, adapt, and grow from it, becoming complete in themselves and not needing another to balance them, their relationship will

develop into a more enriching one. They will be in a more fulfilling relationship that includes greater acceptance of one another.

When you are ready for another partner, rather than looking for the other person to make you complete, you will surely want to be a whole, vibrant, resourceful person in your own right. When you can become that person, you will attract another with the same completeness for an equitable and healthy relationship.

For some, it is a scary prospect to be such an independent person, particularly for those who may have been in a marriage for decades. But you can do it. And you are meant to do it. We will look together at how you can make this a reality.

Why It Is Important To Take Responsibility for Yourself

We looked at why you are only responsible for yourself (plus young children and pets if you have them) and how important it is to put yourself and your self-care at the top of your priority list.

For people who are naturally very caring, this can be a hard one to come to terms with and to find a healthy balance. Those close to you, family, friends, partners, ex-partners know you well. They likely know how to push those buttons that trigger you to take the action they want. You can feel manipulated and used. Manipulation is a sort of emotional blackmail, and when it happens, it's time to look at that guilt again.

Let's turn it around and look at it another way.

Chapter 22
Let Go of the Story

Your thoughts, feelings, and emotions all resonate at a certain frequency and vibration. When you tell the story of your past, you tune into that specific frequency, like a familiar radio station. This is unwanted for a number of reasons, but first, the unpleasant memories make you feel bad. Second, thoughts of the past put you in a negative mind loop in which you keep repeating the same thoughts over and over, and the energy gets stronger and stronger, like rolling a quickly growing snowball.

When this happens, you not only start resonating at the same frequency as in the past, but you actually can attract similar energy to you. This is why people tend to repeat unwanted relationships again and again. If you keep talking about the things you did not like in the last relationship, you will call them in again because you are recreating that same vibration every time you talk about it.

A part of us will always want to try to fix the past by bringing up old stories, but there is no changing what has happened. You can only shift the energy of this present moment to make sure you create a better future.

When you find yourself thinking of something that happened in the past or reliving a story, remember the saying and use it like a mantra. Say: Present moment. Forward thinking. Or Distractor! Distractor!

This will bring you back to this moment and shift your thought stream in a new direction. If you knew the intensity of the flow of energy you are using to think about the past, it would amaze you. When you are able to shift all that energy into the present moment and direct it toward where you would like to go, your life will move forward faster than you imagined.

Sometimes we focus on the past because we may be afraid of what comes next. The past, even if it was a crappy one, seems safer than an unknown future. If you are like most of us, though, you are afraid of the future only because you are afraid you may repeat the past. We repeat the past only if we keep thinking about it. Therein lies the cycle.

There are many organizations that advise us to "remember the past, lest we forget."

Let's consider the word remember: to re-member means to put back together something that has happened in the past.

A more productive way to create a better future begins by visualizing a better future. Think about what you want, see it clearly, and then take the steps to make it happen. The same goes for your next relationship. Visualize in your mind's eye what you would like to experience, then go one step further and bring up the feelings you would like to feel in this new relationship. Bring them up every day. Feel them as vividly as you can. Have as much fun as you can. Talk to your future partner, have fun with them, go for walks and talk to them. Imagine what it feels like to be together.

This brings you into the vibration and frequency of what you wish to create. When you are in the frequency long enough, you become a magnet for that same frequency to come into your life. Eventually a new partner won't be able to help but come in, and when they do, it will feel easy and natural, like they have been with you for a long time. In essence, you have been in each other's same energy and frequency for as long as you have been calling it to yourself.

Built-In Keys to Freedom

Each chakra holds a key to freedom. Each placement of an energy cord will tell you exactly why you connect in the way that you do, and how you can create wholeness in the places that were filled with other people's energy. When we are lacking, or feel that we are lacking, we will try to fill those places with something outside ourselves, usually a partner. This works for a while, and we feel full and complete, hence the phrase, "You complete me." Sure, okay, your partner does complete you, but it's like a patch job. Think of it as an energetic fix-a-flat that can of compressed air you put in your tire if you have a flat so that you can get to the nearest gas station, where your tire can be truly fixed.

Does it work?

Sure, it does, but is the fix sustainable?

No. Eventually you will need to use another fix-a-flat can or you have to get the tire fixed.

Can someone constantly fill you up so that you feel full?

Sure, but eventually they will start to feel depleted, and you will start to feel yucky, because when you count on getting your energy from another person instead of the Earth or Divine Source, you will eventually run out. Humans are not a good source of energy. They become tired, are unreliable, and will eventually resent that you get all your energy from them. The truth is, you don't need to get it from them when you can simply tap into your own energy source.

Why do I mention this?

When you are holding on to someone else's energy because you are afraid to let them go, you are most likely doing this for one or more of the following reasons:

1. You are afraid that if you let go of their energy you will never feel love like this again.

Do you really feel that love right now?

Or are you feeling pain because you are remembering that you once did feel love, and now you are holding onto this pain and pretending you are feeling love?

And if you keep holding onto this energy, you will never find love again because there is no space for you to welcome another person's love.

2. They gave me this energy so now it's mine.

Is this true?

Does it feel like your energy?

If it were your energy, why would you say it was someone else's energy?

Someone else's energy is never going to be your energy. You can feel it, you can take it in and swish it around with your own energy, but it will never assimilate into your field because it is not yours. It's like getting a blood transfusion with the wrong kind of blood. Eventually it will stagnate and keep you from accessing your own energy and power.

3. They need me to hold on to this for them. I am helping.

No, you really aren't. No one can heal something that is not theirs. We all have lessons to learn in this lifetime, but we cannot learn someone else's lessons for them.

You may believe, "Oh, that poor person, let me take their burdens from them so they won't have to go through that anymore." But there is a reason they picked this lesson, whatever it is. They picked it so they could learn it and get to the other side, so if you take this away from them, they will usually recreate the challenge anyway until they understand whatever the lesson is. In the meantime, you have an energy in your field that is not serving you and you cannot heal it, because it's not yours to heal. When you return this energy back to the person it belongs to, they will feel a burst of energy, and they will know what to do with it. It's a gift all the way around. If you still don't want to give this energy back to them because you are afraid it will burden them, then give it to Divine Source. Divine Source will know how to help them better than you can.

The same goes for energy cords.

1. I need to keep this cord attached because we are soul mates.

This is not a healthy life partner cord. This is a cord of fear. The connection you have with another person is eternal, and you don't need a cord for that. We establish these cords out of fear of losing the other person.

Think of the energy cord as putting someone on a leash. You want to hold onto the leash so they will not go away, but the interesting part is that if you truly release the cord, you will probably feel closer to them. You will be able to see them clearly as a person instead of someone you need to hold on to for dear life. The cords warp your connection and cause more of a needy, clingy energy. If you are able to release the cord, you will feel more peaceful and so will they.

2. If I let go of this cord, I will be alone.

Don't you feel alone right now?

The lie we tell ourselves is that this cord keeps us tethered to another, so we don't have to be alone, but it is actually doing the opposite. It is causing us to look to another person to feel complete and connected. Ultimately it will only make us feel sad and alone, because the connection you are looking for isn't actually with another person. It is with Source Energy. We sometimes misidentify human connection as Source connection. And then we get mad at the person because they are not giving us everything we need. In truth, it's not their job. It's our job to connect to Source energy to fulfill our needs.

If your ex was constantly telling you they needed space, yet you hardly spent time together, chances are that they had too much of your energy in the energy field around their body. If you find yourself thinking about your ex constantly and obsessively, it is likely that you have their energy in the energy field around your body.

Having someone else's energy in your energy field can feel really good in the beginning. It's fun and energizing, but eventually what happens is that it slows down and stagnates, and you begin to feel gunky. When you look inside to figure out why you feel gunky, that person is the first person that comes to mind. The reason is not because they did anything wrong specifically, but because you have their energy floating around in your energetic space.

However, another person's old stagnant energy only feels gunky to you because it is not yours. Once you release it back to them they will feel a burst of pure energy, because it is energy that is resonant and perfect for them. The same goes for you. Once you call your energy back from wherever you left it, you will feel a surge of energy because you will be getting back energy that is specifically for you.

Chapter 23
Becoming the Best, Me

Building Self-Esteem and Self-Worth

It's now time to focus all your attention on you. Here, the focus is building you up and reinforcing a positive self-image. It takes a lot of hard work and commitment to work through grief. To combat all the exhausting emotional challenges and hard work you are doing to heal, it is important to balance your healing process by reinforcing and building your self-worth and self-esteem. It is important that you are able to feel good about yourself. If you are having trouble feeling good about yourself, there can be many reasons for this. It could be that you've always struggled with feeling confident or good about yourself, or maybe because of the failed marriage your self-worth has taken a plunge. Sometimes, after a failed marriage, you can become critical of yourself and blame yourself for the marriage not working. If your ex-husband left you for another woman, this might cause you to feel bad about yourself if you compare yourself to her.

Let's think about you, who you are, and who you will become. Thoughts can be powerful and life changing. Therefore, it is vitally important to control what you think about yourself and what you say about and to yourself. We will focus on the following action items that you will use to reconstitute and encourage yourself:

- Replace negative self-talk with positive thoughts

- Speak positive and self-soothing affirmations to and about yourself

- Create a vision board

- Get out and meet new people and do new things

- Create a "Count my Blessings" list

- Keep yourself healthy and take care of your body

It is easy to get in the habit of thinking negative thoughts or saying negative things about yourself and not even be aware that you are doing it. For instance, if you make a mistake or forget to do something or say something incorrectly, you might tell yourself, I'm so dumb. Or if you forget your work laptop at home and not realize it until you get to work you might tell yourself, I'm so stupid I can't remember anything. You might walk around thinking I'm always making mistakes. They are going to fire me. You may not realize how often you make these types of statements to yourself. But the more you speak negative things to yourself, the more ingrained they become. Too much negative self-talk can affect your mood.

Begin reprograming your thinking by replacing negative thoughts with a positive substitute as soon as you recognize yourself thinking the negative thought. You should practice talking back to these negative thoughts so that you can replace them with positive, rational thoughts. You must do this throughout the day, every day. If you tell yourself something long enough, you will start to believe it, and if you believe something, you will begin to act out what you believe to be true. You will need to track all the negative thoughts you have about yourself by writing them down. You can use a journal, notepad, or your computer to keep track of these. It is important that you stay consistent with this in order for it to be effective. Decide on a writing strategy that is easiest for you to maintain every day over the next several weeks or even months.

Make two columns and label them "Negative Thoughts" and "Positive Rational Response." By recording your automatic negative thoughts and replacing them with positive truthful thoughts, you are training yourself to think positive things about yourself. Repetition + consistency = permanency. Here is what it might look like. Example: I can't believe I forgot to pick up the milk from the store. I'm just worthless. I can't remember anything. This becomes Stop. I am valuable, and I remember lots of things. You can even list a couple of things you remember, like setting your alarm at night.

Self-soothing affirmations are good because these affirmations reinforce positive things you already believe about yourself. Work to reinforce positive beliefs that you already have about yourself. Things like, I am a good cook and people enjoy my food. I am a loving person and have some good, positive friends in my life.

In your journal you should be recording your grief work and your affirmations:

- Record how you are feeling each day as part of your grief work.

- Negative self-talk and the positive rational response you used to replace it.

- Daily self-soothing affirmations.

Meeting New People

Begin thinking about getting out and meeting new people and making new friends. You can join a new group or club; take a yoga or Zumba class or take a continuing education course. You can meet new people in these types of settings. Broadening your social circle and Interacting with new people allows you to discover new things and move out of your comfort zone to explore new things with new people.

Treat Yourself

Treat or pamper yourself by doing nice things for you. Think about what feels like pampering and then plan some pampering time at least once a month. If you have time add in a few more in the month. You might consider going to a spa and getting a massage and enjoying the hot tub and sauna. At home you could take a nice bubble bath with a few candles around and the lights dimed. Have some of your favorite music playing and your favorite beverage and relax and enjoy the moment. Treat yourself to a movie or a delicious meal at a nice restaurant or do both. Go to a concert or to see a play or to an opera. Treating yourself is about doing things you like. I've given you a few ideas, but you can use my list and add some of your own ideas to it. Remember it should be a treat; something you don't do regularly. Make it special and select something that will make you feel good. It's all about you!

Count Your Blessings One by One

Make a list of all the things you are thankful for, no matter how small. Sometimes when you begin to reflect on what is going well in your life, you can drown out the loud, negative thoughts that want to tell you how nothing is going well for us. Things like, I am thankful for a roof over my head because some people are sleeping under a viaduct fighting off rodents. Or I am thankful that I am able to think sound thoughts and dress myself each day. These are blessings we often take for granted, but our lives would be extremely different if we did not have them. Choose something small or something big it doesn't matter just make sure you choose something. Create a list and when you are feeling kind of down, think about all the things that are going well. Add to this list weekly and read it

Reinforce Your Affirmations

Another thing to do is to speak your affirmation to yourself when you're driving in your car or doing housework, while taking a relaxing bath, and as you are falling to sleep at night.

Keep Yourself Healthy

Staying healthy is very important and you may tend to ignore your physical health if you are not thinking clearly. The stress associated with divorce can manifest surprising ways. Pay close attention to what your body is telling you. Some of the stress symptoms are headaches, stomach problems, and rashes, muscle aches, grinding teeth that can lead to dental cavities, tweaked muscles, and heart palpitations. Watch out for these symptoms and take some time to address them. If they persist, make an appointment to see a medical provider.

Journaling

Continue to record what you are thinking and how you are feeling each day so that you have a way to evaluate and reflect on what areas in your life are still unresolved. Including the positive rational responses to your critical self-talk, allows you to maintain a balance as you heal and move on with your life.

Chapter 24
Act, Don't React

One of the most difficult things to do when dealing with someone who is making you miserable is to resist the urge to make that person miserable in return. It's even more difficult when you know all of the buttons to push that will set your spouse off. Unless you stop your spouse's misery (or at least stop intentionally causing your spouse's misery), your own misery will never end.

Not making your spouse miserable seems like the opposite of what you should want to do while you're going through a divorce. Many people actually stay up at night trying to think of things to do to make their spouse miserable while they are going through a divorce. What those people don't understand is the law of karma. What goes around comes around. When you do something mean to your spouse, your spouse reacts by doing something mean to you. Then you get hurt, so in turn, you do something else to hurt your spouse. Then your spouse hurts you back. On and on it goes until you're both writhing in pain. If you like being in pain, that's fine. If you don't, then you have to stop inflicting pain on your spouse. Like it or not, that's the only way you stand even the tiniest chance of being able to stop bringing down the pain on yourself.

The next thing you need to do in order to make your life easier when dealing with a difficult spouse is to stop accepting the pain your spouse sends your way. Understand that just because you stop causing pain to your spouse does not necessarily mean your spouse will stop causing pain to you. Your spouse might stop causing you pain or might cause you less pain. On the other hand, your spouse might not stop doing anything at all, and may just continue doing whatever it was that he or she was doing to make you miserable. Either way, just because your spouse causes you pain doesn't mean that you have to take it.

If your spouse is screaming at you and it's making you crazy, leave. Walk away and let your spouse scream alone. If your spouse threatens to destroy your family photos or other sentimental items, get the ones that are important to you out of the house. If you spouse wants to destroy the rest of them, either get those out of the house too, get a court order stopping the destruction, or just let your spouse go. (Which is not to say that you won't ask the judge in your case to compensate you for your spouse's destruction.) If your spouse spreads horrible lies about you to his or her family and friends, as much as you can, let it go. No matter what you do or say, you are never going to convince your spouse's family that you are a wonderful person and your spouse is a dirtbag, so why worry about it? Take the high road. Let everyone believe what they want to believe, and don't waste your time and energy worrying about it or trying to convince your friends and family that your spouse is the one with a problem. They'll figure it out eventually.

Not accepting the pain your spouse sends your way goes hand in hand with not accepting the guilt your spouse tries to lay on you. Regardless of whose fault it is that the marriage ended, the truth of the matter is that both you and your spouse played a role in getting married, and both you and your spouse are responsible in some way for getting divorced. Even if the divorce was mostly your doing or is mostly your fault, feeling guilty about it for the rest of your life serves no useful purpose. What's more, even though you should not try to cause your spouse unnecessary pain, it is not your responsibility, or even within your power, to make your spouse happy. That's your spouse's job. Going through a divorce is rarely a happy time for anyone. If you want to feel guilty about getting divorced, you can. On the other hand, you can also do what you need to do to get over your guilt and get on with your life.

Action, not reaction, is the key to your own happiness. If you want your life to change, start acting in a healthy way and stop reacting in anger or frustration. Stop trying to make your spouse miserable and start trying to make yourself happy. Focus on yourself, not your spouse. Rearrange your priorities. Do what's best for you instead of worrying about what's worst for your spouse. Then let the rest go. It's a subtle shift of attitude, but one that makes all the difference.

Chapter 25
Transform From Being a Victim to a Victor

The moment you decide to look at your relationship with honesty—accepting both your mistakes and your partner's—you transition to feeling like a victor from being a victim. Your partner cheated on you, and that is the choice he or she made over the relationship and which you have no control over. Since you have no control over it, it is only logical that you try to accept it and move on. It is also where you retain power and control by not allowing your resentment and anger to take control of your life.

It is not to say you will never experience bitterness and anger of the past hurts and the lies that surround your spouse's cheating, but you can, however, control how you manage your anger instead of holding on to the angry feelings and replaying images in your memory that keeps you angry. You can redirect negative feelings and thoughts and focus on something more constructive.

Negative thoughts will drain your energy and hold you as a hostage of the past bad experiences, as they keep you from being in the present. But the good news is that there are ways or things we can do to overcome these negative thoughts. For example, you can meditate or do yoga. You can also surround yourself with positive-minded people, smile even if you do not feel like it, sing, list things that you are grateful for at the moment, and help someone else. Helping another person, in whatever way, will help shift your focus away from the pain that you are going through.

Confront Infidelity Wisely

The feeling of anger toward the guilty party is unquestionably warranted. After all, a huge relational injustice has occurred, and the affected partner venting just how disappointed and infuriated they are reasonable. However, if the relationship or marriage has to survive the affair, both parties have to get beyond the cheating and rebuild their relationship, and this means that the berating from the offended partner has to subside.

Having been discovered, the cheating partner may feel motivated to offer you support and compassion for what they put you through. If you continually and punitively shame their action, humiliate, and demean them, it can seriously damage their ego. This might only make things worse. They might find themselves lacking emotional support because of your unmitigated attacks.

Sometimes, having the courage to share what is beneath the anger, for example, is priceless. Explaining how devastating the affair has been for you, how you are heartbroken and hurt, and not knowing how to overcome it allows you to unload the baggage and start your journey to healing. Such words are a genuine admission of sorrow and vulnerability, and they are not about furiously criticizing the offender but giving them feedback as to how harmful their behavior had been to you. Such an assertive admission is more likely to draw the guilty party to confront their betrayal and begin showing empathy and compassion directly.

Take Full Responsibility for What Happened

If you are the cheating partner, begin by owning up to what you have done. It will not be helpful to try to fudge the truth, lie, or justify what happened. Explain to your partner about what happened clearly and acknowledge that you made a terrible mistake and that you are responsible for the choices you made. Do not try to put what happened on your spouse and anyone outside the relationship, such as the other person in the affair. It is possible to feel like you had good reasons to have an affair, but it is helpful to realize that you have control over the choices you decide to take.

Decide to Trust Your Spouse Again

Rebuilding trust in a marriage after a case of infidelity does not happen overnight. It is a slow and progressive work that will take its time. Deciding to trust someone who betrayed you by having an affair with another person may sound impossible, but it is possible. And it is the best thing to do for your marriage if you are keen and determined to restore trust after infidelity.

When infidelity takes place, the partner who felt betrayed feels as if he or she could not trust again. However, with no trust between the partners, there is no relationship either. Therefore, if you decide to stay and rebuild the relationship, restoring trust after infidelity is the most important step of all.

So, to revive trust and rebuild your relationship, you have to come out of the loop of replaying the episodes of the affair in your thoughts. You need to break free and take small steps toward resurrecting your marriage after an affair.

Sever All Ties

Say you are the partner who was involved in the affair. You have to know that there is no chance of restoring trust if you try to maintain some form of communication with the person you had an affair with. You have to cut all ties to the relationship as soon as your spouse discovers the affair. You cut contact by not talking to them on the cell or via text. You quit interacting online, and most of all, you quit seeing them. That is if you intend to work on your relationship. The affair must completely come to an end if your goal is to restore trust in a damaged relationship. Let the other party know in crystal-clear terms that it is over and inform your spouse that you have ended it or that you are planning to do so immediately.

The cheater needs to make sure that there is no further contact with the person they had an affair. Avoiding making contact, perhaps, is the most difficult thing to act on and implement. But for the sake of your marriage or relationship, you must do whatever you have to do to make it impossible for the two of you to communicate again. It could mean changing your cell phone number or the email address. It could also mean removing them from your social media, such as Facebook. An extreme situation is to skip town if it is necessary. You need to do this to ensure that there is no further contact, which can lead to more involvement.

Stay Present-Oriented

One difficult thing about restoring trust after being cheated on by your lover is staying in the present and focusing on the future, rather than living in the hurtful past. It is only natural to feel angry, hurt, and sad about the decisions your partner made, and you have every right to feel them all. However, eventually, you will have to let go of those feelings and focus only on the present and the days to come for a chance to re-establish trust. This course of action also allows you to work toward a more positive and open approach to the marriage. But if you can't let go of these feelings, it may be a sign that it is unworthy to stay in the relationship any further.

Trust Yourself

This is yet another important but difficult thing to achieve in a relationship after an affair. At this point, you might be starting to question your instincts. Maybe you think that you should have done some things differently or that you saw this coming. However, becoming aware of all the factors contributing to the partner's infidelity and moving forward are two important things in having a healthy relationship. It is important to understand that cheating is not an excuse to abuse your partner. Your spouse still deserves to be treated with respect.

Infidelity in marriage and relationships can cause some serious damage to people. Anger, bitterness, heartache, depression, and betrayal are feelings that can lead to resentment. However, if the goal is to salvage the relationship, your partner must learn how to manage these feelings and find ways that he or she can use them to restore and build trust in the relationship again.

Trust is not something that you earn; it is given. Any attempt to try and control your spouse, instead of trusting and respecting them to make their own decisions, will create unhealthy power dynamics in the relationship. It is not an easy job, working toward a healthy relationship, and trying to restore trust after cheating. It is a confusing experience, and I encourage you to try and use the above guidance to manage resentment while restoring trust in your relationship after infidelity.

Chapter 26
Secret to Happy Marriage

Admit We Have a Problem

As best you can, before the conversation heads into a sixty-minute fight, take your spouse's hand and invite him or her to sit down on the couch to discuss something that is weighing on your mind. Say to your spouse that you have made a mistake and you take ownership for this mistake. Say you know this mistake affects both of you as now you are alone, disconnected, blaming, and finding fault. Share that you both are being defensive of your positions. Share how you feel hurt, angry, and disconnected, and ask how he or she feels about how you fight when a problem comes up. Ask your spouse if we can both take ownership and responsibility regarding our part in contributing to the disconnection.

Admit We Both Feel Hurt

Next talk about the hurt you are feeling about how you two argue. Communicate and say you feel sad and hurt in how you two communicate anger and blame. Ask your spouse, "How do you feel about how we are arguing?" Explain to him or her you feel hurt, and empathize how your spouse probably also feels hurt. For example, maybe the hurt reflects disrespect. Can you say to your spouse, "I feel hurt because I feel disrespected, and I imagine in the way I talk to you, you also must feel disrespected? Is that what you are feeling?" The goal is to express how you both feel hurt and are affected by the way you are talking and treating each other. Share with your spouse that you do not want to blame or find fault anymore, as this only brings hurt to the marriage.

Admit the Effects on the Marriage

Third, talk about how these hurts are affecting not only you as an individual but the two of you as a couple in how you talk and treat each other. Say something like this: "When we fight like this, I feel sad because I hurt you, and instead of us loving one another, we are being mean to each other." Share and be vulnerable how these unhealthy intentions affect the marriage. For example, maybe you are sleeping in separate rooms, finding ways to avoid each other, and feeling tension being around each other. Share how you sense both of you tend to walk on eggshells around each other to avoid another fight. Take ownership and admit what you have done now and in the past, to contribute to being disconnected and feeling alone in your marriage. Be honest and confessing, not blaming and accusing. This will begin the process of building trust and emotional connection.

Share Your Desires

Share with your spouse what you want and what you desire for the two of you. Share with your spouse that your hope is for the two of you to find a new way to resolve conflict so that both of you can relate in a much healthier way. Say to your spouse: "What I really desire is that when a problem arises, we both respond and not react with unhealthy intentions which only lead to distance." Ask your spouse what they desire and want for the marriage. Discover and discern how the two of you can participate and learn what you desire for the sake of conflict resolution.

Share Your Needs

Share with your spouse what you need. Maybe you need words of reassurance that your spouse will be there for you. Or share your need for comfort and empathy. Your needs are very important, and it is important to tell your spouse what you need in the moment. Say to him or her, "Honey, what I need are words of kindness when a problem or mistake happens in our marriage. I have needs, and you have needs. Can we find a way to meet each other's needs and not just solve or identify the problem? I don't want us to keep doing what we have been doing, because I feel insecure and scared, as we both just don't like each other anymore, and this leads to the fear that you will leave me or not really care about how I feel. I need for you to listen to my needs, and I will listen to your needs. Maybe if we express what we need, we will find a way to meet each other's needs and enjoy each other rather than blaming each other." It is a beautiful thing to get into the habit of asking your spouse, "What do you need from me?"

Value Apologizing

When was the last time you apologized to your spouse for your part in what you contributed to a fight or argument? Do you find this uncomfortable, or do you resist because your pride gets in the way? To apologize means having to be humble and swallow your pride for the sake of confessing and admitting your part in what you did and how sorry you feel for contributing to mistrust, hurt, and pain. To apologize also means to show empathy and compassion to your spouse by really being sorry for bringing hurt and pain to your spouse. If you can take the lead and do this, then maybe your spouse can also learn to do this for the sake of the marriage, recognizing how the hurt or pain has now affected the marriage.

Apologizing may or may not heal the hurt; some hurt does take time to heal. But at the very least, if you can apologize, you can say with words and expression how sorry and compassionate you feel for bringing hurt to your spouse and to your marriage. Say to your spouse that you know just saying the words can help, but you also know that healing the hurt may take time, and you understand this process. This saying is not true: "Love means you never have to say you are sorry."

Preserve the Good

As best you can, find a way to hold onto what is good about your marriage. Even when you and your spouse are arguing, focus on how much you feel loved and how proud you are of all the two of you have done in the years together and share this with your spouse. The principle is this: Don't let any fight or argument sabotage the good you have going in the marriage. Count your blessings and be grateful for the areas in which you have a good marriage. Tell your spouse that despite this current conflict, deep down you do love and care for your spouse, and you do choose "us."

Practice Forgiveness

When you are ready, try to model and practice forgiveness. To forgive someone is to cancel the debt or mistake they made that hurt you and hurt the marriage. To forgive is to say to the person: "You don't owe me anything, and I am not going to hold onto this memory, or this fight and use this hurt as a weapon to punish you later." When you are ready to forgive, you are not only doing this for the marriage, but you are also doing this for yourself. To forgive is to let go and not participate in holding onto resentments, grudges, and hostility. When two people find a way to forgive one another, they stop being stuck and find a way to move on. This does not mean you forget, and it does not mean you will get over the hurt right away. But at the very least, you do want to practice forgiving.

Pursue Reconciliation

To reconcile means both spouses can say what they have learned from an argument and what they are going to do differently next time as a way to keep building trust, closeness, and intimacy again. Seek and find ways to pursue trust, and as trust builds, both of you will feel more comfortable letting down your walls of self-protection. To reconcile is to return to the "we" and become close and emotionally connected again for the sake of desiring intimacy.

Learn How to Give

Look for ways to fight for your marriage, moving from hostile accusations to caring acceptance; learn to show acts of love, kindness, and care toward your spouse. Let me unpack what I mean.

In general, there are three ways in which spouses express either hurt or love towards each other: taking, getting, and giving. Everyone expresses each of these attitudes at times, but if you constantly take or get, you will remain stuck in your unhealthy marriage. When we take, we make the marriage all about ourselves, find ways to criticize and control, and look for ways to bring up and hang on to resentment. What do I mean? When we take, we look at each conversation or encounter with our spouse and take what we believe belongs to us. Someone with a taking attitude views their spouse as theirs, giving themselves permission to control, criticize, correct, and demand ideal expectations.

A second attitude is getting. A lens of getting views each conversation or encounter as a means to get something. Each transaction is like a sales transaction in which someone gives in order to get something back. Givers give to get. For example, we may give love, acceptance, encouragement, or forgiveness, all the while looking for an exchange. It's easy to view giving as a condition: I give to you; you give to me. Getting something becomes the motive behind giving. Again, this is unhealthy and hurtful for your marriage. A healthy marriage does not look at each transaction with the intention of taking or getting, trying to manipulate or coerce your spouse to participate in the game of take and get. A marriage is not like a retail store in which I give my money in exchange to get an item. But that can't happen in your marriage.

So, the final attitude of what breeds and feeds a healthy marriage is when two spouses choose and want to give. Spouses who give love, acceptance, encouragement, and mercy deeply desire to want to express love in the form of giving. Givers have in their hearts compassion, empathy, kindness and understanding which motivates them to want to give. They give these gifts of love with no strings attached just because they love you. Givers give favors the receiver may not deserve but do not feel obligated to give favors based upon some owing system. Givers give generously.

Look for ways to give, not to take or get. Takers look for ways to justify their accusations, getters look for ways for fairness wanting an even exchange, and givers give with no strings attached. Pursue and fight for being a giver and give healthy intentions generously. If you notice your spouse consistently taking or getting, find a way to discuss this, and if you can't, find a good therapist to work with you and your spouse to have conversations in which both spouses want to move from accusing each other to accepting one another. And I promise, as you do this, your marriage happiness and satisfaction will be till death do us part!

Chapter 27
The Need for Partnership

Marriage is a partnership between two people. People form partnerships because they want someone who can help them to fulfil specific goals or dreams. It could be something as simple as the goal of companionship, or something as complex as fulfilling a lifelong dream. Couples need to establish what they both want to achieve on a day-to-day, week-to-week, month-to-month, and even year-to-year basis and then help each other to achieve it.

Partners are chosen because of what they contribute to a union. They are also chosen for their strengths. Because a husband is a man and a wife is a woman, let's look at the strengths of the two different genders. In these politically correct times, people are trying to blur the lines. But political correctness hasn't improved our relationships or reduced our divorce rates. I personally say that women shouldn't be afraid to be women but celebrate their femininity. And men should have the courage to be real men who are ready and able to take up their responsibilities. A husband and wife form an effective partnership when they bring together and combine their respective strengths.

Strengths found in men:

- Protectors
- Physically stronger
- They're able to look at the big picture which helps them plan for future events
- Sperm-carriers
- Logically oriented

Strengths found in women:

- Nurturers
- Careers
- They're able to look at the small picture which helps them deal with day-to-day events
- Child-bearers
- Emotionally oriented

Of course, this is not a conclusive list. Also, some of these strengths are shared between men and women. But its purpose here is to give us an idea of some of the things that each member of a couple should be aware of bringing into their marriage.

Partnership Outweighs Feelings

When counselling couples going through difficult times, I see that many of them are living as two separate people in one house. Each of them is living their own life and they simply come together at the end of the day or at weekends. There is no fellowship or partnership between them. So, when it comes to the crunch they don't see any reason why their marriage needs to continue. This usually happens to couples who got married based only on how they felt about each other without any common goal or purpose to pursue. So, when the "feelings" faded away, they were left with nothing else to hold them together.

It is a vital marriage strengthening principle to understand that your responsibility to each other is to combine your strengths and forms a fellowship (or partnership) that will help you achieve your lifelong dreams and goals.

Did you ever watch the film "The Lord of the Rings: The Fellowship of the Ring"? That film is a beautiful illustration of this concept. Nine people formed an association with each other because of a common goal, disposing of the evil ring no matter what it cost them. Each of them had a part to play. One had the responsibility of being the ring bearer and the others had the responsibility of protecting him and being his companions in the journey. The ring bearer Frodo had a friend who was willing to give up his food and even his life to ensure that their goal was accomplished. A very touching scene near the end of the film shows Frodo being carried by his friend because he was too weak to walk to the edge of the volcano into which the ring had to be thrown. This depicts the responsibility that husbands and wives owe to each other, which is to form a fellowship based on their common life goals.

Partnership Reduces Conflict

So many of the couples I've counselled and observed couldn't seem to grasp how fundamental the concept of partnership is to their marriage. I easily see this when they play games and "score" points against each other. Think about a soccer team that has 11 players all working together to make sure that they score a goal. One person may score the goal, but all of them work together to make sure that he does. Each player has his own talent, strengths and abilities and he brings them to the team to makes sure that he does what he needs to do for that goal to be scored.

If they would remember that they are partners on the same team, working together to score goals that are mutually beneficial, a lot of the bickering would cease. How many basketball players would throw the ball into their basket? How many football players would knowingly score a goal against their team? If a player does it once, you would probably say that it's a mistake. But if it becomes a habit with him, you would know that there was something definitely wrong. If couples would really understand that they're on the same team, then they wouldn't work against each other, but for each other and a lot of the arguing and quarrelling would cease.

Partnership supports the sharing of household chores and responsibilities

A wife told me about the talk she had with her fiancé prior to their wedding. He had been brought up as one of the older boys among several sisters within an African culture. As a result, he wasn't in the habit of doing any housework or helping domestically. During the discussion, she said that she didn't think that it would be fair for both of them to go to work Monday to Friday and she would still be the only one to do all the housework, cooking, and childcare.

He thought about what she said and decided that it wouldn't really be fair for him to expect his wife to work the same hours as he did and still have to bear all the burden of the housework. He couldn't ask her not to work because financially they needed the input of both salaries for the plans they had. Now after several years of marriage, he shares the household chores with her and sometimes does quite a bit more than she do. His family is still surprised whenever they visit about how much he's changed. They planned to share the household work as partners with various responsibilities and workloads.

Many couples don't plan for this before they get married and it becomes a real issue afterwards.

When couples are conscious of being life partners, it would reduce the instances of independent and selfish behavior from either the husband or the wife that reduces the feelings of love that couples have for each other.

Chapter 28
Seeking Help

When we found out that we were cheated on, we felt like the world was crashing down in on us, a tsunami of shock and inaudible sound that flattened itself around our ears.

Depending on our personality and the circumstances around how we found out, our reactions may wildly differ from person to person. Inevitably, however, we all went looking for help elsewhere, even if that help exists solely in the form of a sympathetic and hopefully helpful book.

This extends to every aspect of the relationship following the discovery of infidelity. The quality of the advice we seek need not be infallible; that is too much responsibility to place on any person. It does, however, absolutely have to be fair and honest. Even friends with biases (I hate your husband) can be sources of enormous help if they're open with you and themselves about their bias (I hate your husband, but if you want to make this work, I'll grit my teeth and support you any way I can. I promise not to set fire to his car).

We just had one rug swept out from under us. We don't need to lean on someone else unreliable. Remember, while the latter problem is likely nowhere near as devastating as our partner's actions, it can very well have horrible practical consequences. Think, for example, the result of confessing our deepest sorrows to someone only to have them confront our partner with a blow-by-blow of the same. They may have good intentions, but the road to hell is paved with good intentions, too, so take this advice and stay the hell away from people like that.

Family can often be a double-edged sword where support is concerned. Often, we'd have those furious on our behalf, and it can be refreshing to have their constant support behind us. On the other hand, we may also find those willing to take this as an opportunity to deliver a poorly timed I-told-you-so, or snipe at us, or use us as fodder for gossip. To be clear, our friends and acquaintances can do this too. It just tends to hit a bit harder when the family is responsible. We should be wary and keep in mind that being family doesn't make them any less human. They can be as kind as any other person, and just as cruel.

For now, let's say, however, that we've exhausted our social and familial circles for individuals we can rely on. This is not to say we don't have any. It could be that we've leaned on them hard for an extended period, and we're concerned about wearing away their goodwill, or even just avoiding taking advantage of their good nature. It could also be that they're too close to us and our partner, making it all but impossible for anyone to have an opinion we can trust, objective or otherwise.

The solution, of course, is to seek help from strangers.

That's not to say we should walk out the door at the crack of dawn and consult the first jogger with a questionably tiny dog we see — not that kind of stranger. We ought to go hunting within that vale of dreams and nonsense, otherwise known as the Internet. Just remember that the online universe is very much a reflection of humanity itself, so exercise caution there as well.

We might dip a toe in and type in a google search for how to get over someone cheating on you. Results will vary depending on where the user and where the search is initiated, but in general, we should receive results from a variety of sources, ranging from psychological studies to magazines to blogs.

Factually speaking, the articles based on psychological studies are the best when looking for statistics and other information. For example, five minutes of googling may lead us to the news that a person that has cheated once in a relationship is three times more likely to cheat in the next one. If we are the 'next' relationship, that may give us more incentive to act now and get out as cleanly as we can. Knowledge is power, and a little experience can go a long way in a pinch.

A couple more tips here: Use more than one website. It's always good to see where the experts disagree, and which aspects they agree on more often because this is an indication of how reliable information is. Oh, and beware of websites posturing as professional sources. There are no one-stop, three easy steps, get-there-do-this methods of getting through the emotions piling over us. As with everything worth doing, we've got to do the work, and we've got to do it right.

We're also likely to find someone telling us how to stab our partner/ex-partner's tires and allegedly get away with it. There will almost certainly be questionable parties encouraging more severe forms of revenge. Do not do that. These are crimes, and we shouldn't forget that we would be the most likely suspect following a breakup.

Also, it's wrong. If asked, mention this first!

That's not to say magazines and blog posts don't have their place in the post-cheating conversation. Professionally sourced articles are noteworthy for their objectiveness and their factual reasoning, but they can also come off as pretty dry reading material. Digesting facts and figures are already tricky enough without adding stress and heartbreak to the equation. A heartfelt blog post or an article written by an experienced writer looking out for their readers can do wonders to get us on the right track, or even suffice to lift our spirits.

Then, of course, we shouldn't discount online support groups and forums. There are various places online where we can log in anonymously, to vent our frustrations and talk to others going through tough times like we are. These places can be a fantastic haven for a variety of reasons. First of all, as long as our username isn't "FirstNameLastNameBirthday," there is anonymity. No one will know who we are and nothing we say will be connected to us. It can be a great way to vent our frustrations. Secondly, online support groups and forums are filled with people who have gone through or are going through a situation similar to ours — people who will empathize, understand and support us. We have to make sure we go to a good support group – or that we don't mistakenly enter a support group for an entirely different issue. It may not be easy to see the value in these online communities at first, but time should tell whether they are worth it. Third, the internet doesn't have opening hours. Whether it's the middle of the night or the crack of dawn, we can log in and talk to someone. The responses may not be immediate, but there is an undeniable therapeutic advantage to having a place to immediately vent your anger or worry or frustration without bottling it all up.

Hey, even reading about fuzzy animals can help. Whatever works, works. Don't knock it just because it seems unorthodox. Seek ye respite where ye may, as the saying goes.

And if that isn't a saying, it certainly should be.

There is also a wealth of resources on video sites that serve this purpose, running the gamut from professional to amateur. If sitting back and digesting what someone has to say is more our preferred style, that's a great option too.

Nothing has changed, though. It still feels like there's a hole in our chest, and now our family is getting worried about the way we've been late to work all week. About our lack of appetite. About our self-imposed exile from social events.

Couples therapy can often feel like a big step, but, in our case, we do have something of a silver lining. Since the indecision to go to therapy together is often over admitting to ourselves that something is wrong. Well. We're dealing with a case of infidelity. We're a bit beyond the point where we wonder whether we're blowing things out of proportion. If nothing else is working, if arguments keep rolling in, if communication keeps grinding to a halt, couples' therapy may be what we need to get things moving forward again. Remember how we talk over the value of an objective opinion earlier? There are few opinions more aim than a medically qualified professional.

The biggest issue when our partner cheats on us is not necessarily the act itself. It's not the fact that our partner was intimate with someone else that bothers us; it's more the betrayal of trust. We've talked about. That painful shattering of faith is what proves the hardest to get part in most cases.

We should note that just seeing a marital therapist or psychologist is not a guarantee of being able to salvage our relationship. However, if correctly approached, the therapeutic process can help us make substantial steps towards that goal. Of course, as we've talk over earlier, this is only an option if we want to rescue our relationships.

Whether we're staying together or not, the help of a knowledgeable professional can help heal the wounds, defuse our anger and allow us to move past the Incident.

Another note: Mileage may vary from therapist to therapist. We must be careful to choose a therapist that both our partner and we are comfortable with. There are also differences between psychiatrists, psychologists, and the like. The former is geared more towards the medication side of things, which is probably not what we want if we're dipping a toe into counseling. Research the type of doctor needed; they will likely openly advertise themselves as couples' counselors if that is their specialty.

There's also the undeniable advantage of confidentiality. We never have to wonder whether the things we share will ever leave the room like we might when confiding in loved ones. As much as we love and trust them, that fear is always there;

while it may never abate altogether even with a therapist who has a legal and ethical obligation to keep our inner thoughts to themselves, it still likely is less intrusive.

If that doesn't seem like enough, remember that we have been going for the better than nothing approach, since this whole thing started. We want a world where our partner hadn't done what they did, too, but here we are, dealing with it as best we can. We need professional help sometimes. Whatever works, works.

Following all this, we may have some answers to our burning questions and insecurities, but we shouldn't feel discouraged if we don't. The beauty of seeking out help is that it's sometimes enough to have it to feel supported in a time of personal crisis. That feeling is invaluable all on its own, even if it appears to be functionally useless. We're looking after our emotional well-being, too, after all.

It also has one more benefit. It gives us a resource to pull from when we gather ourselves to deal with everything that happens as a result of our partner's transgression. Fair or not, there's always more that we have to deal with.

Chapter 29
How to Invest in the Marriage

Positive Interactions

When we talk about positive interactions, it does not have to describe big positive events. It can be as small as a supportive comment, say a compliment, or express appreciation for something your partner did. Saying a sincere Thank you. Offering him/her assistance with a task. "Can I bring you a tea?", "Can I help you fold the laundry, wash the dishes etc.?"

Expressing appreciation and gratitude is particularly powerful. Tell him or her thank you for something they did today, yesterday, even if it was three months ago (if you must go back that far). Just mean it, don't fake it, please. It won't work.

Caution: Do this without expecting an immediate thank you and a reciprocal expression of gratitude. This is critical to remember. Don't screw up a good moment by expecting a proverbial "pat on the back" immediately - even if you already made 5 investments. This mistake is more common for men.

How "Withdrawals" Happen to Your Investment

Likewise, negative events can be represented by something as (seemingly) insignificant as a judgement at how your spouse handled the discipline of a child, criticism over being late to an appointment, a spending decision you disagree with etc.... or as a snide comment about their clothing.

Of course, you have the right to state your opinion; just keep in mind that the ratio reality will impact the relationship. So, keep on dropping in positive and affectionate investments in your spouse. This will ensure that the balance after you make a negative "withdrawal" will insure the maintenance of a loving and intimate relationship.

Practice doing this exercise and reap the benefits.

Dedicate Couple Time

Set time for Date night. Simple. Make it happen, without waiting for the perfect moment. It can be eating out, a movie, just going for a walk, an oom drive, whatever... The main thing is that it is just you two and it is a special time.

Why is this important?

It keeps flaws, weaknesses, mistakes and conflicts from threatening the relationship. It helps protect against feelings of contempt and resentment for your significant other despite how dumb you think they are. These kinds of feelings tend to develop after a few years of being together and knowing each other's faults, flaws and weakness. They are threatening to a couple's love and friendship and are a major cause of divorce. This system tells you that your partner and relationship are still worth holding on to.

Exercises to Reinforce the Paradigm change (to be done together)

This will help you revive or nurture your fondness and admiration for one another

Talk about your history; how you met, what attracted you to each other, memories about your dating period, why did you decide to get married, your wedding day experience, how your honeymoon was and so on. You can also talk about past difficulties you went through and how you got through them together – and why you stayed despite certain challenges.

On different sheets of paper, list each other's positive qualities. Match every quality with a specific event, where they displayed it. Exchange the sheets and watch your partner's face light up.

To put this in perspective. The love map is an exploration of the individual needs. This exercise, on the other hand, is a reinforcement of the shared experiences together. This also serves to help put the ratio issue in perspective. When you are going through a difficult time you can use this to recall magical moments of Happiness together fondly. As you become more vulnerable and emotionally intimate with each other you will develop the ability to decide, in middle of a serious disagreement/misunderstanding, to look at pictures of a vacation, in order to assist your Paradigm change.

It gets better with time. Start today!

Create a Love Map

Acquaint yourself with your partner's world; get to know your partner.

Marriage brings us together as one, but it is wrong to think that just because you are married you both share the same dreams, personal goals, likes and dislikes, fears or aspirations. When we think this way, we don't really bother to discover our significant other. Most times we assume we know them because either we are in a relationship with our partner since college, know their family or you are both "so passionately in love" that you cannot possibly be missing anything. As a result, we lose out on really understanding and connecting with our partners.

There is and there will always be more that you know about your significant other. You can always try to get to know them better, and you can do this by enhancing your love maps.

Love Maps

A love map is a space in your mind reserved for storing all the relevant information about your partner's life. So, how detailed is your love map is another way to ask, how well do you know your partner?

We all change overtime, married or not. You cannot expect that the person you married six years ago is the same person now. We all grow and develop, and in the process we may embrace new interests and passions, have better or bigger dreams, change the way we see things (perspective) and so on. The following example explains this better:

A husband knows that many times when his wife was upset, she brightened up when he brought her flowers or wrote a card and put it under her pillow. Things might have changed over time. She might be more interested in talking about issues that bother her instead of being distracted by flowers. This might be particularly true if she's disturbed about something that he did or said. His gesture of affection may be rejected because her need is to "talk", instead of getting flowers. Taking the time to find out about your spouse love map pays off in a royal way.

Love maps help us stay connected, which is important to sustain a happy marriage. It helps you keep your partner happy and enhances intimacy and friendship because you know what they want, what makes them tick and the things that upset them; you are less likely to screw up mistakenly. If we do not keep connected, we will always be irritating one another; and someday we glance at the person sleeping next to us and wonder who this stranger is.

How to Build Love Maps?

First, you need to designate time for exploring the Love Map. What you do with that time will depend on your individual preferences and circumstances.

Chapter 30
Choosing Happiness

Have you heard the saying, "You can be right, or you can be happy?"

That saying is a truth bomb and in my opinion, it's worth unpacking.

You might respond by saying "Why can't I be right and be happy? After all, being right often feels gratifying and triumphant and is therefore a feeling to aim for, isn't it?"

Well, yes, however, if you are in a relationship and you are focused on being right, what that usually means is that your partner needs to be wrong. For most people being right implies that other viewpoints, feelings, and experiences are wrong. Among people who accept the value of multiple points of view this need not be true. However, it's easier to grant other points of view in academic settings and business contexts than it is when making important decisions with a spouse or in the midst of conversations about painful subjects.

There are actually two distinct issues with being right: The first one is related to making your partner wrong. Being right can be gratifying in the short term, but ultimately it works against you, because being wrong is not sexy at all. If you think your partner is wrong on a regular basis, you are likely to find it difficult to be attracted to him. Who could be attracted to someone who is constantly wrong? Respect, admiration, and erotic heat are not readily available in a relationship where people are regularly and habitually finding each other wrong.

The other reason that being right undermines the health of your relationship is that it comes from a place of certainty, which is the opposite of being curious. Being right is a form of close-mindedness and creates barriers to real connection.

You might think the goal of a conflict is to win, but it isn't. The real goal of a conflict is to understand both yourself and your partner better. It allows you to see what matters to you, and it provides a context to reveal mismatches between your values and your experience.

One of the best illustrations of the importance of choosing to be happy rather than being right is in the Hindu legend known as The Six Blind Men and The Elephant. The story goes like this:

After hearing about elephants at length, six blind men finally have the opportunity to touch one. Each blind man reaches out and feels a different part of the elephant's body. The one who feels the elephant's leg says an elephant is like a pillar. The one who feels the elephant's tail says it's like a rope. The one who feels the elephant's ear says it's like a fan. The one who feels the elephant's massive side says it's like a wall. The one who feels the elephant's trunk says it's like a thick snake. The one who feels the elephant's tusk says it's like a spear. All six men have complete conviction that they are right based on their respective experiences. Indeed, each is correct in his evaluation and yet each of their experiences of the elephant are unique!

Choosing happiness is an essential quality of conscious partnership and yet this skill is sometimes misconstrued as acquiescence or suppressing the truth of how you really feel. This has been referred to as spiritual bypassing, where you opt for happiness without ever addressing the thing that wasn't working for you. That is definitely not what I am talking about here. Instead, it is the prioritization of curiosity, honesty and kindness by the people in the relationship. Built on such a foundation, choosing happiness leads to empowerment, freedom, and personal power. This power can be used to navigate any kind of wonderful or challenging situation.

Choosing happiness is an invitation to make an internal shift that you can access at any time. It is a simple choice that is always available and can be employed to improve any moment, requiring only personal agency and fortitude.

I first explored the skill of choosing happiness when I was a full-time mother, with three young children at home. I loved being a mother and I loved being at home, however, my patience and inner reserves were routinely worn out by the end of the day. Wanting my children to clean up their toys, while making and then serving dinner, were not my happiest times. My husband would come home, and I appreciated the support, but still, I was stretched too thin and had a shorter fuse. I watched myself become resentful and I didn't like it.

After all, this was my life and I wanted to enjoy it! There was no one who was going to help me at home so I could take a few hours off on a regular basis to rejuvenate myself. We were not in a position to go on romantic dates as a way to bring more joy into my home and into my marriage. So instead, I needed to figure out how to make our everyday lives more erotically charged, I needed to figure out how to choose happiness.

I enjoyed experimenting and bringing my creativity to the challenge. One day, as I cooked, I slowed my movements while sautéing vegetables. Another day, I did provocative hip circles as I washed dishes. I took the time to savor the smells filling my kitchen, and treated the pretty designs on my dishes inherited from my grandmother as art. I felt my apron moving back and forth along my body, in flow with my feminine movements. I naturally breathed more slowly and more deeply. My voice lowered and my heart opened.

One evening, I sat across from my husband at our dining table. Instead of looking at him as a co-parent here to help me herd our brood, I looked at him and made a point of seeing the handsome man he is. I let myself have the internal experience I might have if I saw him sitting at a bar. I felt my genitals soften and moisten, and I swayed my hips ever so slightly in my chair as I served pasta and chicken.

The most amazing aspect was to feel delight in the mundane. It was completely gratifying. I was never going to eliminate the mundane while raising young children so finding a way to really enjoy it was a premium discovery. On top of that, I noticed an immediate and positive impact on my whole family. My husband was more present and responded as a person does when feeling seen and received as a whole being. I had shifted from treating him as a co-parent to my sexy man who was collaborating with me in parenting our children.

With this change, my children were also more at ease. They listened more, they were more patient with one another, and quickly became altogether more enjoyable. Our dinner conversation was engaging and dynamic, and the mood consistently pleasant.

I never said anything to achieve this wonderful transformation. What I did was no more and no less than shifting where I put my attention, what my priorities were, and how I felt inside. I chose happiness and the results were magnificent.

I urge you to find your cup of tea. It should be something that lights you up and might even feel a little naughty: a feather boa perhaps, a sly looking hat, heels, or a bit of red glossy lipstick, playing sultry jazz at times of day that used to be challenging…the options are limitless.

A prerequisite to choosing happiness is clearing your resentments and doing so on a regular basis. This guarantees that choosing happiness is not a form of spiritual bypass; you are not sidestepping your resentments because you are clearing them first.

There are many ways to clear resentments. It's best to commit to a method you resonate with and will also use consistently. Physical methods include vigorous exercise, yoga, or being in nature. Emotional methods include receiving bodywork or expressing how you feel to a trusted friend, therapist or coach. Another option is to write letters to whomever you resent (without sending them). Hypnotherapy, Byron Katie's "The Work" and similar modalities can also help. Meditation and prayer are spiritual ways. This list is not exhaustive, and no one way is better than another for clearing resentments. Anything that helps you release stuck feelings of anger, grief, resentment, sadness, feeling misunderstood or unimportant are excellent ways. Once you let such feelings go, you have the internal freedom and inner spaciousness to begin to choose happiness more often.

One of the most common pitfalls that couples face when they are in challenging times in their relationship is focusing on what isn't working. Typically, by the time a couple seeks professional guidance, they will be very focused on frustrations in the relationship and the ways their needs aren't being met. This often leads to forgetting what's actually wonderful about the relationship. The exercise at the end four invited you to look at what you love about your partner and the ways your relationship has already been serving you. Now it's time to identify some reliable ways for the two of you to enjoy yourselves while spending time together. The Fun Activities List is designed to be a resource for achieving just that! When I met my clients Deborah and Shane, they were in a toleration relationship. They didn't actually have much conflict, but they certainly didn't have passion either. They made love once every six weeks or so, but it wasn't really satisfying to either one of them or sometimes it was easily a few months between times. I assigned them the Fun Activities List exercise and suddenly they found themselves laughing together more often, flirting as they hadn't in years, and really enjoying one another's company. This naturally led to more erotic energy between them and without any other efforts besides practicing curiosity, sharing honestly, and being kind, they went from each preferring to be on their own in the evenings to looking forward to being together at the end of each day.

Chapter 31
Turning Conflict into Ways to Grow

Take a moment and think about the first time you met your spouse. What struck you about him or her? Was it their mannerisms, the way they looked? The way they smiled. Look at your spouse now. What still strikes you about him or her? Is it different than when you first met?

As you get to know your spouse, you both grow and learn more about one another. Your initial response to them may be a thing of the past. After a few conversations with them, you may find that you enjoy their personality and sense of humor much more than you had remembered.

Conflicts are a normal part of any relationship. Some conflicts can be good. You learn that something that you once thought was fine really isn't after all. By learning where you are wrong and taking responsibility for your wrongs, you are growing as a person. You may never know what you are doing wrong until you have an unavoidable conflict.

Knowing what you love about your spouse will help you to keep focused on the end result of the conflicts that will arise during your time together. If all you focus on is the problems of your marriage, then you will lack the ambition to save your marriage for the right reasons. Resolving a conflict in a civil manner is nice, but it's also nice to know that the person on the other end of the conflict still loves you for who you are and what you stand for. That is a valuable feeling to carry with you.

As a couple, you want to learn to grow together. This cannot be done without learning about one another and having some conflicts along the way. Think of conflict as growing pains. In order to reach an end result, you need to get past the worst of the problems and look forward towards the bright future ahead. Taking the time to figure out what is bothering your spouse and how you can fix it in order to make him or her happier is just one way to show your love for each other.

Using your conflict as a way to grow is not only a more constructive way to view it, but it will also help you to resolve it in a more loving and gentle manner. When the focus is off of you and your desires, then the conflicts are resolved in a nicer and much more amiable manner. We are all human and none of us are prefect. Mistakes are going to be made, so why not use these mistakes to make you a better person and improve your relationship with your spouse?

Look At Conflict as a Chance to Learn

Just as people make mistakes and then try to learn from their mistakes, think of conflict in the same way. Something brought you and your spouse to the point where something must be resolved. A mistake needs to be rectified. Taking the time to work through the problem and coming to a conclusion together will help you to both grow and learn.

Don't try to resolve anything by being defensive. This is the worst attitude to have. First of all, it's selfish. You are only out to protect yourself, no matter what the cost. Secondly, you will not be open to seeing your spouse's point of view, which totally defeats the purpose of confrontation. Go into the conversation with an open mind and an understanding mindset. This will help both of you to resolve your differences without the situation turning into a full-blown argument.

If you approach conflict as a way to learn more about yourself and your spouse, then you will find that conflict resolution can take place in a more loving and constructive way. You may have to make the same mistake a few times to learn from it, but once it's engrained in your mind, it will be a memory!

Learn From Your Past Mistakes

Many of us will repeat a past mistake over and over again. It's not that we don't feel bad about what we have done. It's because we are human, and we tend to make mistakes. When you find that a certain method of conflict resolution hasn't worked out in the past, then stop trying to use it. Learn from your past mistakes and move on to your future!

Knowing that you have a conflict to face and resolve can be stress provoking. However, finding a solution to the problem and learning from the situation will help you grow as a person and learn to avoid such mistakes in the future. You may not even realize that you have made a mistake until your spouse comes to you hurt and angry.

Not only should you learn from your past actions, you should also learn from the ways in which you handled the situations in the past. Knowing that lashing back at your spouse in anger is not the best method of conflict resolution will help you to avoid using it when the next conflict comes along. This will help you both home in on the best way to solve your problems.

Put Your Spouse's Feelings before Your Own

Many of us tend to be selfish by nature. It has been taught to us throughout the years to be that way. You have probably heard people talking about looking out for number one. In marriage, it's important to understand that you are not number one. You should save that spot for your spouse. Think about how he or she would feel in any given situation. When you put their feelings before yours, then you won't be as defensive and out to get your way. This will help the solution be more amicable for both of you.

Your spouse should carry this very same viewpoint when it comes to conflict. A loving marriage requires that you put your spouse before yourself. Put yourself in his or her shoes before you even bring up the situation. If you can't do this, then step away from the conflict until you can come back to it at a later time and do it. Your tense emotions may stop you from putting your spouse's thoughts and feelings before your own, so learn to talk about them when you are both calm and rational.

Growing in your marriage should be top priority. Just getting by isn't good for either one of you. Learn from one another and learn from your past conflicts. Use the past to help you heal the present. Don't dwell on the past but focus on the future. No matter what, we are all students in life, and marriage is no exception to this rule! Learn from your mistakes and use them to build a strong and healthy relationship!

Chapter 32
Re-Story Your Life

Once I stopped looking at my marriage through either a haze of pain or rose-colored glasses, once I began to look at me instead of the marriage, once I completed my marriage autopsy and allowed myself to retrieve the good, I realized that it was in my marriage that I achieved my first bloom. I saw my strengths and my weaknesses and accepted them all as glorious parts of me. Most importantly, I began to find the joy in creating something new, a life uniquely designed for me, by me. The freedom of that was exhilarating. Every step on the journey you have taken thus far has led you here, the beginning of your second bloom.

The writing came first. Because I had journaled most of my life and because it was one of my lifelines through my most wretched moments; I leaned into writing. I joined an organization called the Story Circle Network and in a small online group began to share tiny snippets, just a few hundred words, about my life. I found community and encouragement there. I didn't write just about the betrayal and divorce. Because they provided a monthly prompt, I wrote about my mother and dad, my school, my son, my hopes and dreams. Those stories grew into essays and I gathered the courage to begin to write a memoir. When the memoir felt too big to tackle, I did a course correction, began to write personal essays, and found a literary home there. While taking classes to learn writing craft, I tried my hand at fiction and realized how freeing it was to be in complete charge of how the story unfolds.

Because I was a teacher and had done staff development, I designed a writing seminar called Legacy Writing. It is a six-week course in which beginning writers craft and polish one story into print for their friends and families.

This is how the second part of my dream to help other women crystallized. My therapist and writing mentors suggested I think about life coaching. When I realized it could mean working with women one-on-one or in small groups, helping them develop the skills and confidence to name and pursue their dreams, I felt that frisson, that deep knowing, that this was my path.

I invited my first group of Legacy Writing students to my home to celebrate their "publication," distributing the bound collection of their stories. What a thrill to watch the joy of having a "first book" in hand. That night, I shared this new and very tender life coaching dream of mine. I asked if any of them knew about life coaching and if they thought I might be good at it. To my utter astonishment, two of the women had recently worked with life coaches, and both they and the others in the group encouraged me. Yes, they said, you could do that, and you will be good at it. See how the universe lined that up for me? I became a life coach, to add that to my way of helping others through.

I had been coaching in one way or another for years; it was a through-line in teaching and writing. One sunny day as I was journaling about my coaching practice, I looked up and noticed the amaryllis plant near the window. The plant was a gift from a friend and had bloomed in a spectacular fashion. Once it ceased blooming, I had stopped noticing it. That tall first bloom had withered and was drooping downward, but right next to it was a strong shoot with a second bloom on top ready to burst into its glory. At that moment I knew what my business name was: Second Bloom!

My first plan was to write personal essays and memoir to share my experience to help other women. My first writing goal was essays in literary magazines, and I achieved that, winning some awards and scholarships along the way. The long-term goal was a memoir, which is a work-in-progress. I tucked away an additional dream to publish fiction, showing women a range of new happy endings.

Coaching fills my life with bliss. The beauty of coaching is that it is interactive, and for an extrovert like myself, that is a dream come true. I assist women on their paths to a new life. Assisting other women, coaching them as they create the life of their dreams gives me joy and I am so grateful to be able to do this.

I took a leap of faith, learning a new writing genre. Self-help books are written differently than memoir or fiction but draw in a way from both. This guidebook is my love letter to women poised to recreate their lives, ready to craft their second blooms.

Re-storying your life is like fiction writing. You choose the characters, you create the plot, and you design the finish. It's also like personal essay and memoir in that the building blocks, the growth lessons from your life, are there for you to draw upon.

One of Steven Covey's 7 principles is "begin with the end in mind." So, let's pick an end point to plan toward. Let's start to re-story your life now. One caveat: allow room for surprises, gifts, from the universe. Name your dream, lay down your plans, and take bold action toward them. And at the same time keep an open mind, allow for more.

I am indebted to Angela Laurie for the inspiration for this next exercise. Angela, the book maven who founded the Author Incubator, in one of our coaching sessions tossed out the idea of writing your bio from five years hence. Brilliant! I believe that putting your dreams down on paper is the first step toward actualization. But, as Dr. Phil frequently advises, you have to put some verbs in the sentences.

First, settle into the idea of a five-year leap. Write down the year and your age then. Now visualize your ideal future life. Brainstorm in these areas: family, friends, relationships, health, career, wealth, lifestyle, and achievements. Where do you live? Who's with you? What are you giving to the world? What are your current goals and pursuits? What is your current dream?

Now write a third-person biography for yourself at that time. Hold nothing back! Dream big because this is the you to come.

Chapter 33
Counseling and Therapy

Many victims of narcissistic abuse end up seeking professional help, and if you feel that you need it, you should certainly go for it. You don't need to do this alone, and it might be that your friends and family give you enough support, but still don't quite get to the heart of the issue.

Healthcare professionals are seeing more and more people visiting their clinics and centers who are suffering the after-effects of narcissistic abuse. There are groups set up to help support people like you, and there are countless other men and women out there who can sit down with you and have a conversation that is so deep and completely on your level, because they 100% understand exactly what you've been through - all because they've been through it too.

Sometimes that's all you need, someone to be able to relate from the personal experience completely. Of course, it might be that you need something a little more in-depth, and if that's the case, again, take it.

Counseling, therapy, medical interventions, these are all available for victims of narcissistic abuse and talking to your doctor, or a healthcare professional in general will allow you to access these help methods and look forward to a brighter future.

Post traumatic stress disorder (PTSD) is a form of mental health condition. Someone who has come out of a narcissistic relationship and is so badly shaken to the core by the manipulation and mental and emotional abuse they've been subjected to falls into this category. That doesn't mean you're failing; it means you've been through something hard and you need help.

Many divorcees suffer from depression and anxiety at the end of a marriage, even a marriage which isn't connected to narcissism in any way. It's like a death in some ways; you're grieving the end of something which you thought would last forever, and the realization that it's not going to be can be very hard to deal with. When you add manipulation and abuse onto that, you can understand that the picture can be extremely dark and distressing.

You do not have to go through your life struggling for a second longer; the help is out there; you simply need to ask for it.

Don't Rush Into a New Life

Part of the recovery after any divorce is to give yourself time to heal and recover, but after a narcissistic relationship, that is even more important. You cannot and should not attempt to jump into another relationship simply because you think that's going to block out the memory of the one before.

If you do that, you're simply carrying old baggage into a new relationship and not allowing yourself the time to process what happened and understand the fact that it wasn't your fault. You're more likely to repeat the same patterns of behavior as a result, which will put pressure on your new relationship, making it more likely to fail.

You will not be able to have a happy and healthy relationship until you have processed the events of your former marriage and made peace with it. After that, of course, you have every chance of falling in love once more, but that doesn't mean you have to either. If you want to continue your life and enjoy time alone, that's perfectly fine too. Go with whatever feels good for you.

Another point to be aware of is to avoid jumping into unhealthy habits as a way to mask what you're feeling. Firstly, distraction techniques are never a good idea, because you're basically masking the problem and not dealing with it, and secondly, if you opt for an unhealthy coping choice, such as smoking, drinking, eating too much, shopping, etc., then you're causing yourself another problem on top of the heartache and pain that you're trying to heal from.

For your own good, make sure that you focus on healthy routes forward and learn to handle the pain and the upset that you've been through. There are plenty of people out there who are waiting and willing to help you and to access that help, you simply need to reach out and ask.

What Does The Future Hold?

Life after a divorce can be strange for a while. You had your life mapped out, you thought you knew who you were going to spend the rest of your days with, but suddenly everything changes, and you're left wondering what you're supposed to do.

This feeling is normal and it's something you have to face in order to move on. The world is full of exciting opportunities and these will come to you over the days, weeks, months, and years to come. You will not be able to see them and grasp them in all their positive glory unless you do what we've tried to explain to you throughout - understand and deal with what's happened before jumping into a new life.

Your future does not have to be the same as your past. You have made a huge leap of faith by leaving your marriage to a narcissist and going through the very tough, yet necessary, divorce proceedings. Now, you're free to live your life and understand that you're a wonderful, worthwhile person who doesn't deserve to be controlled by anyone.

Conclusion

What a journey we have followed! When you arrived, you knew you wanted to save your marriage. Perhaps you had already tried several approaches. Or perhaps you were still gathering information, not quite sure where to start. Or perhaps you were still feeling very much lost. I hope you have now shifted to a new place of understanding and action.

At this point, you have a clear understanding of what it takes to both transform a marriage in trouble and keep that marriage on-track.

Remember that knowledge is only one element of the process. Knowledge without action — without courageous action, is worthless information. How are you applying this information? How have you been transformed? How have you been transforming the relationship?

The path to mastery is interesting, for any area. You have been on a path of mastery, both in relationship skills and in personal transformation. Sometimes, we lose track of our progress.

There are several points along that path of mastery:

1) You don't know what you don't know. This is a point of blissful (or painful) ignorance. You don't even know that there is a problem or that there is information you are lacking.

This is the beginning point for any journey. We all start here. That is the nature of life and the beginning point of learning. It is a place where many people remain. And if an area of life does not affect you, it is possible to stay frozen in not knowing what you don't know.

But when something is no longer working, when you reach the limits of the usefulness of the tools you have, something beckons you to make a shift. Sometimes, it is an opportunity or a curiosity. Often, it is a crisis. With relationships and personal growth, it is almost always a crisis that pulls us into the next stage.

2) You know what you don't know. At this point, you have become aware that there are some skills, tools, attitudes, or perspectives that are missing. As you begin to look around, you realize that there is so much more to discover.

If the reason is compelling enough, you take action to learn the new skills, discover new perspectives, and master a new area of life. If the reason is less compelling, you may simply lose interest, overwhelmed with a new body of information.

3) You know what you know. At this point, you are more aware of the skills you have discovered. You can point to the theories, strategies, and techniques you have learned and are implementing. When someone asks, "Why did you do that?" you can provide a theoretical explanation of the reason. At this point, you may still be mastering the application, but you understand the reasoning.

This is likely the point where you are right now. You may have some new techniques and understandings that are transforming you and your relationship. At times, you may be frustrated at the fact that you do not "do it perfectly." But you know what you are striving toward. Mastery of a new skill does not come overnight.

4) You don't know what you know. At this point, you have attained a level of skill that allows you to interact with the new approach on automatic. Your skill level means that you are acting and responding differently without much thought about it.

The difference between Level 3 and Level 4 is only one of practice. What at first feels awkward begins to feel more and more natural. A higher and higher percentage of the time, you respond in the "new" way (which is quickly becoming the "old" way, as it becomes the default). And, you see it working better and better.

Remember these points:

We ALL start from a point of not knowing, of ignorance. It is the ONLY starting point there is.

A change in attitude and behavior takes time, energy, effort, and courage. Doing anything differently is partly a matter of our brain creating a new neural network to replace the old method.

It will always feel awkward at the beginning. Any new skill does. The only thing that makes it less awkward is to continue doing it.

The in-between space — between the old way and the new way, can be frustrating, both for ourselves and those around us. That is a space where you take three steps forward and two steps back, as the old thought processes creep in. Be patient with yourself. Change is a challenge.

The effort is worth it. The cost of staying where you were is heavy and rarely has a pay-off. The new perspective will offer more opportunity of possibility, even if it can feel a little scary.

It is important to reinforce the change by noting the shifts you are making. You can also find other material that reinforces the changes you are making. Growth, once it starts, can continue with just a little effort. Seek out information that broadens your new perspective. But only seek out information as you are ready to implement. Information for information's sake will not lead to growth.

Creating A Plan

At this point, you have the information in front of you. If you are still reading, you know what you need to do (knowledge), you want to make a shift in your relationship (courage), and you have been making some changes (action).

In order to make sure you are staying on-track and do not get pulled back into old patterns of thinking and acting, it is a good idea to be intentional about creating your plan for saving and transforming your marriage.

There are three areas upon which you will want to focus:

Connecting With Your Spouse

What methods, specifically, do you want to use in your effort to connect?

What are the ways the two of you connected in the past?

Think back to the ways you connected as you were falling in love. What actions made your spouse feel loved? (Don't get trapped into thinking about what your spouse did that made you feel loved.)

How do you see your spouse showing appreciation and love to others? (This will give you some clues about how your spouse understands love.)

Make a list of actions, attitudes, and perspectives to which you commit yourself in your attempts to reconnect.

Changing Yourself

What are the areas in life where you have excused yourself and for which you need to take responsibility? (We all have them. We have to acknowledge them, in order to start the process of change.)

What are the actions and attitudes that hold you back and are counter-productive to your personal growth? (These tend to be habits of action and thought that are limiting and even destructive.)

What are the standards you have, that you need to raise to the next level? (Remember, a standard is what you expect of yourself.)

Make a list of the actions, attitudes, and perspectives to which you commit yourself in your growth toward being your best self.

Creating A New Path

Where are the places in your life in which you have not been acting as a WE?

How, in the past, have you responded to fears of intimacy and fears of abandonment? How will you respond, intentionally, in a different way?

How can you invest more in being a WE? (This is about you stepping into being a WE, not expecting your spouse to be doing the same.)

Make a list of the actions, attitudes, and perspectives to which you commit yourself in your efforts to create a new path for your relationship.

Spend some time writing down your responses. This is not just a thought exercise. It is an exercise in intentionality, best done by writing it down and reviewing it frequently.

When we don't write down our plans, they tend to get lost in the busy shuffle of life. We lose track of what we intended to do. With the best of intentions, we end up reverting to old ways of responding.

More than that, saving your marriage is about existing in a world of emotions and turmoil. When the emotions get you, it is easy to forget the plan. It is easy to slide back into the place of hurt and reactivity. That place serves neither you nor your relationship. It is simply the primitive part of your brain that gets stuck in "fight/flight/freeze" behavior.

In those moments, remember a quote my wife often uses:

Consult your plan, not your feelings!

Feelings will lead us away from useful behavior when we are struggling. Your plan, though, is made in a moment of clear-headed thinking. It will keep you on-target and headed in helpful directions.

Made in the USA
Middletown, DE
07 April 2022